Your Identity Isn't Found in Your Pant Size

Breaking Free from the Mold You Were Never Designed to Fill

Title: Your Identity Isn't Found in Your Pant Size
Subtitle: Breaking Free from the Mold You Were Never Designed to Fill

Cover Art: Chelsey Dollman
Cover Art Photographer: Ivan Samkov
Editor: Jana Spooner

Unless otherwise noted, all Scripture is taken from The Holy Bible, English Standard Version. ESV® Text Edition: 2016. Copyright © 2001 by Crossway Bibles, a publishing ministry of Good News Publishers.

Also used: Amplified Bible, Classic Edition, Copyright © 1954, 1958, 1962, 1964, 1965, 1987 by The Lockman Foundation.

Also used: The Contemporary English Version. Copyright © 1995 by American Bible Society. For more information about CEV, visit www.bibles.com and www.cev.bible.

Also used: The Holy Bible, New International Version®, NIV® Copyright ©1973, 1978, 1984, 2011 by Biblica, Inc.® Used by permission. All rights reserved worldwide.

Also used: The New King James Version®. Copyright © 1982 by Thomas Nelson. Used by permission. All rights reserved.

Also used: *Holy Bible*, New Living Translation, copyright © 1996, 2004, 2015 by Tyndale House Foundation. Used by permission of Tyndale House Publishers, Inc., Carol Stream, Illinois 60188. All rights reserved.

ISBN-13: 978 1 990211 01 0

To my beautiful friend Cindy,

for your unwavering faith in God—it is beautiful. And for faithfully praying that this book would answer the cry of a thousand generations of women's hearts to be reconciled to God through loving who He created them to be—inside *and* out.

Table of Contents

Preface

To say writing this book has been a journey of unexpected twists and turns would be an understatement. I began writing this book two years ago, and I have written and re-written it at least three times—from start to finish. I was like the writer you see in cartoons, frantically scribbling away on a pad of paper, then ripping off a sheet, crumpling it up, and tossing it in the trash.

When I first began, I wrestled painstakingly over the words of this book, pouring over them again and again, analyzing and overanalyzing my writing. *Is it too specific? Am I saying what I really mean? Is it too wordy? Do I need to say that? Should I add something there? Is it personal enough? Is it too personal?*

I was surprised by the struggle I had. Frustrations with writing were new to me. Oftentimes, when I sit down to write, it flows freely from heart to hand, but this time was different. It was as if a roadblock was in my way—a mountain of tremendous proportions. But I refused to give up because I had a passion deep within my heart, and I knew I needed to get it right. I knew God had put the passion and words in my heart—it was just a matter of how to get them out. The enemy tried to stand in my way, but God made a way!

God had shared His heart with me, and it was a heart that broke for His daughters. I could feel His heart beckon for His daughters who thoughtlessly tear themselves down, ripping apart their appearance, believing their worth and value are wrapped up in external things.

I sensed His urgency to speak to His daughters with a powerful message, but I struggled to convey His heart from pen to page. I struggled with how to share my journey. I wanted to be raw and vulnerable without glorifying the struggle, but instead glorifying what *God did in me* through the struggle—glorifying Him.

God had pressed a word on my heart that I couldn't let go of: identity. Identity in Christ. Holiness on the inside, who we are in Christ, who we are inside—that's what matters. We have to stop focusing on the outside and let the inside be the vessel God uses. We must learn to give the hurts to Him, the pains to Him, and let Him do the refining process in our minds and hearts to see ourselves the way He sees us. These are the first words I put on paper as God started speaking His message to my heart.

Despite popular belief, God has purpose in the pain. He uses it to bring us from the pit to the palace, like Joseph (Genesis 37–50). God brought me from insecurity in myself to security in Him, from worry and angst about who I was to confidence and peace in knowing who I am in Him.

I wouldn't have arrived where I am without the

journey that got me here, without facing the giants that stood in my way. God promises in Romans 8:28 that He will work all things out for the good of those who love Him and are called according to His purpose. And He's right—He does.

I went through hard things to get here; that is true. But without going through those hard things, I wouldn't be standing in front of you, set free from the bondages that previously held me captive. I wouldn't be confident and secure in who I now know I am.

We like to think we learn through the easy times, but friend, we are refined only through the Lord's redeeming fire in the hard times. Yes, it will most likely be hard when you're in the middle, but on the other side, dear friend, you will shine like a thousand diamonds.

I believe God has given me this word for women of all ages who need to be reminded of their worth in Christ and reject what the culture says about them. God has walked me through the battlefield and brought me safely to the other side. Through each step of the journey, He gave me the battle plan to pass on—a manual to give His daughters the weapons they need to fight the good fight of faith. It's time to discover who you are and who God made you to be in all your intricacies, and trust that He didn't make any mistakes when He formed you—inside or out. Listen and trust His voice as you read through this book—His still, sweet, small voice.

CHAPTER ONE

Who Do You Say You Are?

O ne summer, Queen Elizabeth was visiting Balmoral, her summer home in Scotland. Typically, during her stays there, she enjoyed retiring from her formal wear and royal duties, as well as spending time with her family. This included walking her dogs, playing with her grandkids, and strolling the rolling hills surrounding her fifty-thousand-acre property.

One sunny day, while strolling around the property in her outdoor attire, she ran into a group of American tourists. Upon running into them, the Queen and her head of security, Richard Griffin, began talking to the tourists. Griffin noticed right away that the tourists didn't recognize the Queen. The tourists asked the Queen if she lived around there, and she replied that she did. She told them she'd been coming up to vacation there since she was a little girl, about eighty years. Upon hearing her response, the American tourists responded with amazement and said, "Well, you must have met the Queen then!" Without missing a beat, the quick-witted Queen laughed and replied, "No, but this man sees her regularly," pointing to her head of security, Griffin.[1] The tourists began to pepper Griffin with questions about what the Queen was like, to which he replied, "She can be quite cantankerous at times, but she's got a lovely sense of humour." The tourists then asked the Queen if she would take a photo of them with Griffin—she happily obliged. They then asked Griffin to take a photo of their group with the Queen, still completely unaware of who she was. He did. Then, they parted ways, the tourists without the slightest inclination as to whom they'd just met.

The interesting thing about your identity is w*hen you know who you are, your value doesn't change based on what others think of you.* Queen Elizabeth didn't need to tell the tourists who she was in order to be Queen—she just simply *was*. She didn't need to prove her status or worth, nor did she need their approval to be Queen—she just simply *was*. The tourists being unaware of who she was didn't devalue her position, her crown, her heritage, or her inheritance. She knew who she was, and nothing— no circumstance or lack of knowledge—changed that. Telling them who she was wouldn't have changed anything for her, although it would have drastically changed things for them, I'm sure!

YOUR IDENTITY

Who you are doesn't change based on circumstance or on what others think of you. Who you are isn't fluid (despite what the culture may tell you)—it's constant and it's solid. Your audience may change, opinions about you may change, your circumstances may change, people may like you one day and not the next, and people may say things about you that aren't true, but even then, who you are is who you are—who God created you to be.

The word identity has been assaulted in the current culture. The idea of identity has become something fluid, something changeable, something chosen, something someone else can put on you—a label. It's become both a traumatizing trigger-word and a praised buzzword. It's a word that's both despised and celebrated, depending on the crowd. As per usual, the culture has assaulted something that God made good and skewed it. For the sake of this book, I want you to relearn the original, God-intended meaning of the word identity.

Your identity is that you are made in God's image—both males and females. His unique character is inherent in who you are. Your identity doesn't change—it's not fluid. Your identity can't be chosen—it's given. It's given to you by your Maker, your Creator, your Father. You will learn who you are and Whose you are throughout this book, so I encourage you to re-learn and learn to love the word identity because it's integral to the truth of discovering who you are.

As Christians, we have an enemy, Satan, and he knows that the most dangerous thing for a believer to know is who they truly are, who they are created to be, and the inheritance they have in Christ. The enemy spends so much time and effort trying to make you believe lies about who you are because he knows that if you really understood your identity, you wouldn't believe his lies, and you'd be set free. He knows that he loses his power when you know who you are. He knows that his lies will be exposed when you know who you are. He wants to fill your mind with lies—lies spoken by other people to tear you down or lies that he whispers to you that make you question your identity and worth. He uses many voices to try and make you doubt your true worth and identity, but it's time to stop listening to the lies and learn the truth about who you really are.

Being confident in who you are starts with understanding who God made you and knowing your inheritance because of your adoption into His Kingdom. In a culture that assaults our identity as daughters of the King, we have to have our minds renewed in the truth of who we are.

The culture around us can strip and steal our identity and worth if we allow it—if we let it in. The culture tells us that we need to look a certain way, act a certain way, have a certain amount of money and social standing, and fit into a mold that's nearly impossible. So many are stuck in the trap of believing their worth and value are wrapped up in what they look like. They desire approval and believe their value comes from being accepted based on those material or physical things.

Jesus came to set the prisoners free. We are prisoners when we believe the lies from culture. Jesus came to tell us the truth and teach us exactly who we are. He did this because He knows that once we understand our true value and worth, and accept our identity in Christ, nothing can hold us back from stepping further into truth and being all that God has called us to be. When we know who we are, our worth and value are no longer in shaky external things but are eternally stable!

Imagine a life in which you see yourself—emotionally, spiritually, and physically—the way that God sees you. For a mere moment, believe that you are who God says you are—set apart, chosen, loved, forgiven, redeemed, made right with Him, His child—and see yourself through that lens. Does it change how you see yourself inside and out? If you took off the lens of the world and popped on God's lens, would you see yourself differently?

"HI, I'M CHELSEY. NICE TO MEET YOU."

I didn't know my true identity in Christ for the majority of my life. I always believed my identity was wrapped up in how I looked, what others expected of me, or what kind of life I had.

My life story might be similar to yours in many ways, but the journey I've been on with God has been truly unique. My story isn't a romantic fairytale. It's not riddled with wild car chases or high-rise jumps. There are no shocking twists and turns. It wouldn't qualify for a high-octane, action-filled blockbuster. It's not even likely to draw a crowd on a busy New York street, but my story does have something that will catch your attention: It's relatable. My story resonates with so many other women who have struggled to know who they truly are. My experience connects with women who have struggled to know their worth and value, women who have had the cloak of the culture thrown on their back that tells them they are nothing more than what they look like on the outside, rather than realizing they are royal daughters of the King of heaven and earth.

It took me years to undo the negative messaging of the culture around me and to finally wear my rightful cloak. So often, we are content to wear the ratty rags that the culture throws on our backs rather than step into the royal robes that were designed for us to wear as daughters of the

King of Kings. So often, we're content to frantically scavenge the ground for the tiny scraps that haphazardly fall under the table rather than pull up a chair to the banquet feast and bask in the bounty of the generous spread that God has prepared for us. We settle for mediocrity rather than enjoy the goodness and majesty of our heritage. God has planned a life full of wonder for us —one of beauty, favour, and adoption. But we can't step into that calling if we don't know who we truly are—if we don't know our identity. Like the Queen, we must know who we are to walk with authority in our calling.

I didn't realize that my worth wasn't on solid ground but rather on a sandy, unstable foundation until life's circumstances forced me into a place where my foundation crumbled and was swept away by the crashing waves. As with many things in life, sometimes God orchestrates circumstances that, while hard, force us to face lies we've believed about ourselves that were sitting dormant beneath the surface.

IN HINDSIGHT

My journey with understanding who I am in Christ began in 2019. Before that, I was working at a job I mostly liked, raising a family, and enjoying married life with my husband. I was living a life that, from the outside, probably looked pretty good.

Behind closed doors, however, I struggled with insecurities. Some of them were small insecurities, things like whether I was a good wife, mother, or friend, but there were also deeper insecurities lurking below the surface that hadn't shown themselves yet. We will come back to this place and time, but first, let's rewind.

They say hindsight is 20/20, and looking back throughout my life, I realize now I had always struggled with my physical appearance. I never felt pretty *enough*, thin *enough*, competent *enough*. I was always aware of my appearance and would constantly measure myself against the world's standards of beauty—never feeling like I measured up. Physical comparison was second-nature to me, and it poisoned my heart regularly because I often felt I came up short. Taking care of yourself and your appearance is not a sin, but when it starts to be something you give too much thought (positive or negative) to or something that becomes part of your identity and worth, it becomes an idol, and pride can take root. It can become a thorn, a pestilence—and at that point, it can become a sin. I wasn't intentionally idolizing my body, but by feeling insecure about it and allowing my appearance to be part of my identity, it inevitably became an idol.

Perspective is the lens through which we view things in our lives, and in my twenties and early thirties, although I was considered thin, I never felt like I measured up to the cultural standards. Why I thought I needed anyone's approval makes me shake my head now, but at the time, it was because I was looking for acceptance. Insecurity will always search for acceptance.

Growing up, the messaging of the culture around me promoted thinness as being the ideal beauty standard. Much of that had to do with growing up in a diet-obsessed society, as well as a celebrity culture of extreme thinness.

Not much has changed today (thin is still considered the ideal body image), although there is more focus nowadays on healthy weight and embracing various body shapes and sizes. Back then, however, commercials, ads, and even the talk from the adults around me promoted the idea of attaining a "perfect" weight and the importance of that. It seemed diets and weight were all anyone talked about in the late '90s and early 2000s, which were formative teen years for me. It wasn't just talking about weight; it was promoting an unrealistically low body weight that the culture idolized.

In my late teen and young adult years, I was 5'7" and 120 pounds—a perfectly healthy weight and size, but somehow I struggled to feel like I fit in. I was trying to fit a mold that the culture had placed upon me, and I ignored the unique person God had made me. I didn't think or even know about my identity in Christ; I was only aware of my identity as it pertained to the culture around me, and in that arena, I always felt I came up short.

After having kids, my body changed a little, but I was

still considered in the acceptable weight range by the world's standards. The stretch marks that marred my previously smooth stomach were a new source of disappointment for me, though. No matter how religiously I lathered myself daily with anti-stretch mark cream early on in my pregnancies, it didn't matter. The zebra-striped scars made their way to the surface either way, stretching and marring my skin in a way that made me feel embarrassed. My husband and the few close friends I chose to share it with all told me to see them as battle wounds and to "wear them proudly" because they're scars borne from having two amazing children—a gift that some women never get to experience. I understood that logically, but it never resonated with me inside. It wasn't a healing salve to the insecurity that burned inside, telling me to be ashamed. The scars were just another thing I felt embarrassed about and wanted to hide. They were yet another thing that brought my insecurities to the surface.

My physical scars and insecurities weren't obvious to anyone but me, but I grieved inside, feeling there was no one I could talk to, no one who understood. Back then, twenty years ago, it wasn't talked about from the pulpit, on blogs, or in Christian circles. It seemed no one in the church talked about these kinds of issues, and I felt too embarrassed and shameful to admit I was struggling with something so frivolous as my outer appearance. It didn't feel holy or Christian to talk about my looks or the insecurities I had. I felt as though it was something that would have been considered prideful, yet I wrestled with it. It felt like a dirty little secret, lingering in the background–something I didn't want anyone to know about. So there the insecurity just sat, on the back-burner, waiting to be triggered—always vaguely there.

Unknowingly, I had let my outward appearance become a part of my identity. It didn't start out that way, but as I let the messaging of the world around me define me rather than God, it slowly began to sneak in. Rather than it just being about insecurities and scars, it became about seeing myself only through the lens of my outward appearance. Suddenly, I didn't know who I was as a child of God, but instead, I only heard what the culture around me told me I was. I was another girl caught in the net of the culture that told me my value was based on what I could do, what I could look or act like, or what I could do for others, not who I was.

Fast-forward to 2019.

In November 2019, after trying multiple interventions for seven years, my thyroid was unable to regulate itself, and I had to have it removed. It was a painful and painstaking decision to make. I don't know that I could accurately convey the weight of that decision. My husband and I wrested with the decision for nearly a year, through many tears. We questioned over and over if we were making the right decision. We prayed without ceasing for eight months for healing, but the doctors told us we couldn't wait any longer, and a decision had to be made.

Healing doesn't always come in the immediate, miraculous form we expect, but in many ways, healing did come through the work of the doctors. I was so relieved once it was finally over, and I assumed everything would go back to normal, including my body.

Life did go on as usual—for everyone else around me, at least—but not for me.

As was expected, after the procedure, I needed to go on medication to have a functioning thyroid hormone (something our bodies need), but it was a constant yo-yo trying to figure out the correct dosage. My thyroid levels continued to plummet, and it came with a slew of other symptoms: tiredness, achy muscles, terrible digestion, hair loss, dry skin . . . the list went on and on. But the hardest one of all for me to grapple with was the weight gain. I put on a substantial amount of weight in a very short time, and on top of everything else that I was feeling, it was the last possible thing I wanted to deal with. It didn't matter what I ate or how hard I exercised; all my efforts came up short.

For someone who has always been active and had a healthy diet and lifestyle, I assumed I could fix things with my usual efforts, but continuing on as I always had just wasn't working. Added to that, the stress began to compile when the spring of 2020 hit, along with the infamous COVID-19 virus. It was already a struggle dealing with all I was going through personally, and then the world went into full chaos mode, which added yet another layer of stress.

At this point, you may be expecting me to say, "But don't worry; it all worked out. Everything is back to the way it was!" Sorry (not sorry) to disappoint, but you won't find that ending here. If that *was* the ending you were expecting, sorry to say it's a bit short-sighted. My story isn't about changing God's plan to fit my desired outcome; it's about God changing my heart to fit His. God didn't give me what I thought I wanted (looking on the outside the way I did before), but He gave me what I *needed*— what I never *knew* I needed. He taught me my true identity.

"C'MON GOD, DO IT MY WAY"

Oftentimes, we try to bend God around our will. We plead with Him to do a certain thing for us, to give us what we ask for because we believe it will make us happy. Garth Brooks sings a song called "Unanswered Prayers." He tells a story of running into an old flame from high school and how he had prayed she would be his wife. But God didn't answer that prayer, and looking back, he was glad because she wasn't who he remembered, and he was different, too. Many times, God doesn't answer our prayers the way we want Him to because He's doing what's best for us—we just don't know how to ask for it. We really have no idea what is best for us, even though we think we do.

We are demanding, like the Israelites, asking God to deliver us the way we want, trying to get Him to follow our plan. We don't know what's good for us as much as we think we do. Paul reminds us of this in Romans 8:26, *"And the Holy Spirit helps us in our weakness. For example, we don't know what God wants us to pray for. But the Holy Spirit prays for us with groanings that cannot be expressed in words"* (NLT).

God sees the long-term. Even though we think God should answer our prayers the way *we* want Him to, God is looking for a submissive heart that allows Him to answer our prayers the way *He* wants to—the way He knows best. God isn't narrow-minded like we are. He sees the big picture. He sees the destination. He sees the end from the beginning.

Allowing God to change me as I walked through the valley, allowing Him to take away the things that hindered me from healing and the things that kept me living in insecurity, allowed me to see that His way of doing things was far superior to my misguided requests. I wouldn't choose to go back to how it used to be before all this, even if I could. I wouldn't choose to go back to that insecure, unsure girl because God has changed things in me that needed to change, and He has healed me from negative mindsets and insecurities that were holding me back.

Oftentimes, when we go through hardships, it's because God is bringing things to the surface that have been buried deep—lies that He wants to expose and bring into the light so He can speak truth into the situation. There are many things that we tolerate or wrong patterns of thinking that we let get into our minds that aren't healthy for us. The only way for us to deal with and fix them is to be made aware of them and for the Holy Spirit to take us through the process of working through those things and, in turn, set us free from them.

Through this challenging yet fruitful journey, I have grown and matured in my walk with God. I've grown so much closer to Him, and I've learned much more than I would have had I not gone through it all. He knows the path that's best for us, even if it doesn't look that way when we're in the middle of the process—but He knows.

After all, it's human nature to try and avoid the ditch, avoid the detours, avoid the hard parts, and take the path of least resistance, but if we are honest, it's in those hardships and trials that we learn who we truly are. Have there been battle wounds? Yes. Scars? Yes. But those figurative (and sometimes literal) scars are a reminder of the healing that's taken place. You can't have a scar without a wound, and subsequently, a scar is evidence of healing. My scars are a reminder of the healing my loving Father has brought me through.

Not much has changed on my outside, but *everything* has changed on my inside. Learning who I am in Christ and learning more about God's character has changed how I see myself and how I view my worth, which is no longer based on external things. My identity isn't in what I look like; my identity is in Him. My view has changed on *who* I am because of *Whose* I am. When the things that I thought were important to me were stripped away, God equipped me to deal with the insecurities that lurked below the surface. I wasn't able to ignore it any longer, and after going through the process of dealing with it and healing from it, I wouldn't want to go back to who I used to be. I know who I am now; I know my identity and my worth, and nothing can change that. It's no longer based on my circumstances, and my identity will never change because God never changes.

He's shown me how to get out of the ditch of insecurity, cast off finding worth in the things of this world, learn who I really am, and find freedom from seeking the approval of anyone but God. He did it for me, and He can do it for you! Through the power of my testimony and walking out the principles in this book, I believe you will see God change and heal you, too!

IDENTITIES WE CLING TO

We can wear false identities, intentional or not. We can let our identities become wrapped up in things like wealth, social status, the group of friends we associate with, our looks, our minds, our work ethic, our jobs, and a million other things. These are things the world and culture around us tell us are important, and it doesn't take long for those things to begin to *feel* important to us. If we allow those things to feel important for long enough, they begin to define us, and we make them part of our identity. And therein lies the problem—one we often don't know we have.

The issue with believing your worth, value, and identity are found in external things is that if all of a sudden those things are stripped away, you will feel empty and adrift, as if you've lost your anchor. When your anchor is in external things, it's not consistent or permanent—it changes. When our anchor is in God, it's stable and sure. God is the only one who can teach us who we really are, who He created us to be, and our identity.

IDENTITY IS LIKE A TREE

The tree is a close analogy of what it's like to have your identity in Christ versus having your identity in external things.

The Branches and Leaves

The branches and leaves represent the external parts of us: our name, our job, where we live, our appearance, our wealth, etc.

During the seasons of the year, trees go through many changes, just like our circumstances. Branches and leaves grow and change. Leaves change colour, fall off, and new ones grow. Branches break, other branches grow longer, and new branches are added. With each new season, the leaves and branches look different.

In the same way, the external things in our lives change all the time. Our looks change, our jobs change, our addresses change, our hobbies or passions change, our friendships change, etc. These things aren't meant to be our identity because although they're part of our lives, they're not *who* we are.

The Trunk and Roots

The trunk and roots of the tree represent the internal parts of us. This is where Christ lives, as well as our identity, soul, mind, and heart.

Jesus is *eternal* and *internal*. He lives inside of us, and He is the *centre* of our identity, represented by the *centre* of the trunk. The trunk and roots are sturdy. The leaves come and go with the changing seasons, and the branches break and fall, but the trunk and roots stay steady, holding up the rest of the tree. The storms and weather (external factors) that affect the branches and leaves do not affect the trunk and roots in the same way because they're deep and secure. Likewise, God doesn't change, which means our identity in Him never changes based on what goes on around us—it's a constant, like the trunk and roots.

What's key to note is that the trunk and roots feed the branches and leaves. The leaves and branches cannot function without the trunk and roots—they would die. In the same way, we cannot have our identity in external things because they change constantly and they're flimsy —they die. But when we have our identity in Christ, it feeds all the other parts of our lives and helps us to function within them, while being grounded in our firm foundation—Christ.

When we know who we are, with our identity in Christ, our identity doesn't change because it's rooted in who God is and who He says we are. Our identity was never meant to be in flux or in external things—it's meant to be anchored in God, our constant.

It takes prayer and study of the Word to learn who we are in Christ, but even then, it's easy to get off track in our thinking and forget. It feels like an uphill battle some days because the culture is all around us—we are immersed in it whether we want to be or not. The messaging comes to us through social media, the news, certain circles of friends, fashion ideals, advertisements, and popular culture. It's everywhere, and it doesn't just come at you in dribs and drabs; there's a steady stream of messaging coming at you all the time. And the messaging is not quiet —it's *very* loud, shouting at us, telling us who we should be. The culture tries to tell you what you should look like and what success looks like. It tells you what your sexuality should be, that your identity is fluid rather than fixed, and that you can choose it based on how you feel from one moment to the next. All of these are lies that assault the truth of God's plan and His Word.

The cultural messaging tells us that we need to do a, b, or c to be happy, to fit in, or to be accepted. Rather than affirm who we are as sons and daughters of the King, the culture instead tries to make us believe we need certain external things to be accepted and loved. It's just simply not true, no matter how loud the culture tries to scream it. The enemy uses his cunningness to try to deceive us into believing the lies of the culture rather than the truth of the Word, but what so many people don't realize is that external things constantly change, and they will never completely fill us.

Jesus said, *"I am the bread of life. Whoever comes to me will never go hungry, and whoever believes in me will never be thirsty"* (John 6:35 NIV). He is the *only* supplier of all of our needs, desires, and wants. He is the *only* One who satisfies.

Sometimes, we believe that the current culture and its messaging are new or different from past generations—but they aren't. Throughout the course of time and history, Christians have stood out from the culture around them—we've been set apart for a purpose, just like it says in 1 Peter 2:9, *"But you are a chosen people, a royal priesthood, a holy nation, God's special possession, that you may declare the praises of him who called you out of darkness into his wonderful light"* (NIV). (See also Deuteronomy 14:2.)

The enemy has whispered lies since the beginning of time, since the Garden of Eden, which is precisely why Jesus gave us the words in John's Gospel to remind us that He is the only answer. He was the only answer back then, and He is the only answer now. That is the truth, and absolute truth doesn't change based on culture or time.

Your identity isn't just about how you view yourself; it's about whether you see *who* you are, *what* you are, and what your *inheritance* is because of what Jesus has done for you—not because of anything you've done.

Sadly, so many people live their lives struggling to understand who they truly are or see themselves the way God sees them, so they begin to blindly accept the world's labels for them without realizing it. Before long, it becomes part of their identity. They accept the labels placed upon them, allowing the culture to stuff them into the box of conformity. People sell themselves short when they do that, and you do, too. There are two reasons: First, the world and culture can't offer you anything that will fully or eternally satisfy you—you will *always* be thirsty. Second, God created you uniquely, and you will never fit into the box the culture tries to stuff you into. The world sees one-dimensionally, but God sees you multi-dimensionally—He sees all the uniquely created parts of you!

Sometimes, we accept these false identities as a way of adapting to the world we live in or a way of surviving. Although we aren't supposed to be a part of the world and culture but rather just "living in it," it can be hard sometimes to be set apart (see Romans 12:1–2). At times, we just want to fit in, to be a part of a certain social circle, or be well-thought-of—that's just part of human nature, and the enemy uses that to deceive us into believing we need that.

You can *try* to fit yourself into the box the culture says you need to squeeze into, but I promise you, it will never bring you fulfillment; it will never satisfy you, and you will never properly fit. There is something much greater than what you have settled for. There is a heritage you are missing out on claiming ownership of because you've settled for appeasing the demands of the culture rather than learning about your true identity—an identity that tells you who you are and what you were created for.

Not only are you selling yourself short, but you are also denying who you are and who you were created to be. It won't take long before that thing you thought defined you—once stripped away—leaves you feeling completely empty because your identity was never meant to be in anything but Christ. This is something the culture doesn't understand, which is why the messaging out there is to try to get you to pick a label that you can use as your identity: looks, gender, sexuality, social ranking, jobs—the list is endless. It's like trying to fill a sieve with water—it will never work. It's a temporary, fleeting, momentary attempt to fill something that is incapable of being filled. It will always leave you empty. Christ, however, is constant, stable, and the vessel in which there are no leaks.

The external things that we believe hold our value and worth are smoke-screens, mirages, illusions. On the other hand, what Jesus says about you and who you are doesn't change—ever. How He loves you today is the same as how He loved you from the moment you were conceived and how He will love you until the moment you leave this earth. Your identity in Him doesn't change, unlike the fickle, external things around us. We have to learn who we are to understand what God has given us through Christ.

HELPING US EVEN WHEN IT HURTS

God cares so much about us knowing our true identity and worth that sometimes we have to take the hard road to get there because that's the only way we learn—through the desert is the only way to the promised land. When you are ready, He will (in His gentleness) reveal to you the wounded areas of your soul. He will expose the lies you've believed that have held you captive. He will uncover the mess, rather than let you continue to live in the deception of the enemy that holds you captive.

Jesus experienced everything that we experience because He came to earth as a human—fully man and fully God. He knows what it feels like to have emotions and feelings because He felt all those things when He was here, too. He felt deeply—like when Lazarus died, and Jesus mournfully wept for His friend (John 11:35). Scripture says that God sees and holds all our tears—not one is missed—and He collects them in a bottle (Psalm 56:8).

Although the path to truth may take us through the desert, I don't believe God has an easy time watching His children struggle, even if that's what is necessary to get to the other side. We read many passages throughout the Old and New Testaments of Him feeling sorrow for His people in their struggles (Genesis 6:6; Psalm 78:40). But often that's the only way through, and many times the other side looks like deeper faith, more trust in Him, uncovering pain to bring healing, being set free from bondages, and walking the hard, narrow, rugged path to freedom.

THE PERFECT PARENT

God is the perfect parent, and I know, as a parent myself, there are times when I have had to make decisions that could upset my kids in the moment. I have let them go through something hard rather than rescue them right away because I know they need to learn how to get through it by relying on God. Even though we know that's what they need, it hurts us as parents to watch our children go through hard things. Sometimes, we have to make hard decisions for our kids that result in our (and their) temporary unhappiness in order to teach them or bring about something that will help them in the long run. They may not always understand why, and it may not even make sense to them at the time, but like so many things in life, it's part of the process. The hope is that because there's a solid relationship there and trust in you as their parent, they believe that your intent is for their good even if they don't understand the method to get there.

Oftentimes, we want God to remove the hard thing, and sometimes He does. But not always. During hard and challenging times, I do still ask God to step in and change my circumstances, step in and fix them, step in and heal, step in and make it all better. He doesn't always do it in the way that I imagine it (by removing all the hard things), but He does always answer my prayers to give me the strength to get through it. No matter what His method is, I have to keep going back to faith and trust. Trust in a God who I know has my best interest at heart and who loves me beyond compare. I know He is good, and His plans for me are incredibly good and beyond *my* wildest dreams, so I continue to trust in Him despite the times when it's hard to hold on. He has had to let me go through hard things in my life in order to get to the place of healing the broken parts of me that wouldn't have been exposed without the hardship. I trust in Him because I know who He is, and I know His character (an area that's important to understand and study).

Through my journey with God changing how I saw myself inside and out, I had to let go of my expectations for what I wanted God to do and instead ask Him to change my prayers to line up with *His* will—to let God move my hand instead of me trying to move His.

I wouldn't have been able to experience or hope in the good of it all without faith. I'm sure you're familiar with this passage, but it says in Hebrews 11:1 that "*faith is the substance of things hoped for, the evidence of things not seen*" (NKJV). Faith propels us to hope and believe in something that we don't yet see. *Faith is built and grown in the valleys, not on the mountaintops.* Christian faith is a deep-rooted testing of one's mind, will, and emotions in the refining fire of God. Nothing flimsy or impure can emerge from the flames, only the purest of forms, in order to see the promises of God revealed.

What's beautiful is God's promise that even when we are tested, and even when things get ridiculously hard, He will still work good out of it. That's what I've come to experience in my own life. I have begun to even anticipate and look for His goodness in the middle of it all and eagerly await to see how He's going to turn the hard situations into something good.

While I was wading through the deep waters of this journey of understanding my identity and worth when everything external had changed, I was never once alone; He was always with me, just like He promises in Isaiah 41:10: *"Fear not, for I am with you; be not dismayed, for I am your God; I will strengthen you, I will help you, I will uphold you with my righteous right hand."*

He allowed me to go through the hard parts so that He could do a complete work in me. He helped mend the broken parts of me to become a whole and healed child of God who has confidence and security in who she is both inside and out, *regardless* of the exterior. Wrinkles, rolls, and sags do not define who I am or who God created me to be those thirty-nine years ago in my mother's womb. I am created in *His* image. I am not broken because I'm not thin by the world's standards, nor am I broken because I have stretch marks. I'm not even broken because of all my outer or inner imperfections, but instead, I am whole because I am His—because I am exactly who He made me to be: chosen, irreplaceable, loved, set free, forgiven.

Do I fit the beauty standards mold that popular culture has put on women? Haha, no! But I'm content in knowing that that's not how God measures me, and by God's grace, I'm honoured to say that, thankfully, that's not how I measure myself anymore, either.

CHAPTER TWO

Losing Control

There's a story of a man, Jack, who was out jogging one day:

As he passed a cliff, he got a little too close to the edge, and suddenly found himself falling. On the way down, he managed to grab a branch, nearly yanking it out of the cliff. When he caught his breath, he realized what a terrible jam he was in. He couldn't get up, and letting go certainly seemed to be a poor option. He began to scream, "Hello up there! Can anyone hear me?"

In a moment, a voice returned.

"Jack, can you hear me?"

"Yes, yes, I can hear you I'm down here."

"I can see you, Jack, are you alright?"

"Yes, but, who are you, and where are you?"

"I am the Lord Jack, I am everywhere."

"The Lord? You mean God?"

"That's me."

"God, help me, I promise that if you get me down from here, I'll stop sinning. I'll be a really good person and

serve you for the rest of my life."

"Easy on the promises, Jack. First let's get you down, then we can discuss those."

"I'll do anything, Lord, just tell me what to do, okay?"

"Okay, let go of the branch."

"What?"

"I said, let go of the branch. Just trust me, let go."

There was a long pause, as Jack thought of the offer.

In a moment, however, Jack let out a loud yell. "Hello, Hello – is there anybody else up there?!"[2]

Any other Jacks out there? Yes? You, too? Yep, I have to sheepishly raise my hand on this one. Although this amusing illustration gives us a good chuckle, it's also glaringly introspective into our desire to try and control and perfectly design our circumstances.

In this short anecdote, we can see that Jack struggles with what to do: follow what he can see (carnal circumstances) or follow what he can't see (faith).

He is dangling off a cliff—a real, physical, laws-of-nature problem. Spiritually, we know he has enough faith to ask God to help him. He's even willing to barter and promise everything but the kitchen sink for God's rescue, but trusting God requires trusting in something he can't see, denying the laws of physics, and doing it God's way, not Jack's. God tells him that he can be rescued if he puts his faith in God and lets go of the branch, but he's conflicted by the physical limitations he sees with his eyes that go against the laws of nature. He's conflicted with the rescue plan of God's choice. Jack would rather God rescue him Jack's way—with something he could physically see, like a rope. Even though Jack had enough faith to ask for God's help, he doesn't have enough faith in what he can't see to actually walk it out. His mind cannot comprehend beyond what he physically sees. Sound familiar? Yep, I sheepishly raise my hand again.

How often are we stuck in this dichotomy of being presented with two ways of doing something—God's way or our way, using faith to believe the impossible versus relying on what we see in our circumstances? How often do we go back and forth between the two choices? We know what God says in His Word, and we often sense what God is saying to us in our hearts, but sometimes, we struggle to look past the realities or complexities of what we see going on around us. Suddenly, it doesn't seem so clear-cut. Suddenly, we are more focused on seeing our circumstances for what they are (the carnal reality) than being willing to rely solely on our faith. Our feelings or emotions rise to the surface, and we are confronted with the choice of following our feelings *or* following God's voice. It boils down to a choice between the two. It's not one *and* the other; it's one *or* the other—*part-time obedience won't work.*

Let's be real, though. Following what you can't see can feel scary because we are often torn between seeing our carnal circumstances, which are very evident, versus exercising our spiritual faith, which is unseen. These two are often at war, but when you know God and His character, it should be easy to trust Him, right? It *should* be easy, but somehow, it's not as easy as it sounds. Feelings and emotions have strong pulls on us, but we *must* learn to overcome making decisions based on our emotions and instead follow God's voice. It takes decisiveness, practice, and a lot of the Holy Spirit's help.

STEADFAST FAITH

The story of Abraham perfectly exemplifies this dichotomy. This passage of Scripture reminds me of what God can do regardless of the circumstances and how we can believe in the impossible with God.

God promised Abraham a child. God said the child would be Abraham's biological child, and he would be the father of many nations. However, when God made this promise to Abraham, he and his wife were very old, far beyond child-bearing years (about one hundred years old). Abraham could clearly see the reality of his situation (carnal reality)—his old age and the *"barrenness of Sarah's [deadened] womb,"* in other words, Sarah's inability to have children (Romans 4:19 AMPC). But he still hoped and believed with faith (spiritual trust) that God would do what He said He would do, even though it looked completely impossible in the natural. That is some powerful faith: to see impossible circumstances in front of you and still continue believing God will come through! And He did!

God is not limited by our carnal, earthly, or fleshly circumstances; He works immensely far beyond what we can see and perceive. He is the God of miracles and the God who makes the impossible possible. We can look at situations with our earthly or carnal eyes, but we will never see the things of God come to pass in our lives if we choose to believe what our earthly eyes see instead of believing in faith what our spiritual eyes (our soul, our spirit, and the Holy Spirit) see. Yes, our circumstances might seem impossible, and we may not be able to see how God could make impossible situations possible, but God will always do what He says He will do.

Believing in what's easily possible requires almost no faith, but believing in the impossible requires much faith in God, and as it says in Hebrews 11:6, "*Without faith it is impossible to please God*" (NIV). Why do we need faith to please God? As it says further in verse 6, "*because anyone who comes to him must believe that he exists and that he rewards those who earnestly seek him.*" This verse reminds us that faith is required in our relationship with God. We show Him that we love and trust Him when we put our faith in Him, regardless of how impossible the situation may seem. It's the highest form of praise to our King.

For example, have you ever had a situation where you are trying to convince a friend or family member of something, and they are unsure if that thing you're saying is possible? You find yourself telling them, "Don't worry, just trust me!" I know I've said it many times: to my husband, my kids, friends, and many other people. It makes complete sense to *you* that that person should trust what you're saying when *you know* it'll work out, without any doubt. However, they often don't know what you know or see what you see, so for them, it's challenging to blindly trust you. However, if there's enough relationship built there, oftentimes, that person is willing to go out on a limb and trust what you're saying because they know your character and that you wouldn't try to mislead or harm them.

When that person does finally agree to trust you with what you're saying, it further establishes a bond between the two of you, and it builds confidence in your relationship and in what you say.

The same is true for God. He sees all the things we don't see, and He knows all the things we don't know, because He's God. He's omniscient (meaning He knows everything). He can see the end from the beginning and the possible from the impossible. He sees the things that come before and the things that come after. He sees everything from the big picture to the small details, so when God says you can trust Him, *you can*! And the more you trust Him, the more your bond with Him grows.

He will always come through. You can take Him exactly at His Word, even if it doesn't seem to be the least bit possible or the least bit probable. And I would add an asterisk to that by saying He will do it *when we trust in Him.* If we are full of doubt, I believe it can hinder us from seeing it come to pass, not because He can't do it, but because doubt is an open door for the enemy. All that to say, when God tells you to do something or that He will do something, surge forward in faith that He *will* do it! Take Him at His Word, just like you want your friend or spouse to take you at your word when you say, "Trust me." Thankfully, though, God is much more reliable than we are, even on our most confident of days!

BELIEVING IN THE IMPOSSIBLE

It's easy for us to look at the reality of our circumstances and see them as they are, but do we still continue to hope in God for the impossible? Do we have hope and faith like Abraham? Do we believe in faith that God can do what He says He will do, even though our circumstances seem impossible? Or unlikely? Are we playing "faith roulette," where we gamble with believing that God *could* do it, but *will* He?

Bill Johnson, founder of Bethel Church in Redding, California, says in his book, *Dreaming With God:*

> *Not understanding is OK. Restricting our spiritual life to what we understand is not. It is immaturity at best. Such a controlling spirit is destructive to the development of a Christ-like nature. God responds to faith but will not surrender to our demands for control.*[3]

As much as we'd like to at times, it's not for us to decide what God will do in our lives. We are not God, and we don't know what we actually need, despite pride rising up and telling us we know best. We need to surrender ourselves—our mind, will, and emotions, to Him. Surrendering to God is giving up control. Surrender means praying for what you feel led to but trusting God for the *right* result—in His omniscience and sovereignty—but with full surrender to let Him do it His way. It's praying for *His* will in any given situation.

WHAT DOES CONTROL HAVE TO DO WITH IDENTITY?

Let's be real: We are human, and as humans, it's easier to get hung up on what we see (carnal) and what we feel (our emotions) than it is to rely on faith. The carnal is somehow easier to acknowledge and harder to ignore. Faith, however, is unseen, and the outcome is not guaranteed because we don't know what plans God has for us other than He tells us His plans are for our good (Jeremiah 29:11). As humans, part of our nature is to want to control our circumstances and be in charge of our outcome, often becoming control-freaks. We don't like the feeling of change or uncertainty, so to avoid feeling that way we try to control things. It may be controlling food, how our bodies look, our finances, the way we keep our homes, our relationships—there is no limit to the areas in which we try to control the outcome.

However, control can be a dangerous, slippery slope. Once you start down the path of control, you're more likely to add to the list of things you try to control than to drop some. Control seems alluring, desirable, even Siren-like, calling us into what we *think* is a safe place.

Control appears innocent and appealing, like the Sirens of Greek mythology, luring unsuspecting sailors to the shore in order to shipwreck them on the rocks hidden below the surface.

To add another analogy, control is like a wolf dressed up in sheep's clothing. It seems innocent enough on the outside, but danger lurks inside. We assume that control will set us up for happiness, orchestrating the outcome we want, but does it? Do we have as much control as we think we do? If we are realistic, very little is in our control. Control is, in fact, an illusion.

When someone has gone through a traumatic

experience, it's common that post-trauma, they will begin to exhibit controlling behaviours in that area. For example, a child who was bullied in school may withdraw from other friendships, hoping to avoid more pain. If they were made fun of for their looks, they may even try to alter their appearance in some way in an attempt to control the situation. It stands to reason that the terrible emotions they experienced during the trauma are not feelings they want to experience again. Feeling out of control is one of those uncomfortable emotions, and if they can't control the trauma, they either try to control something in their life related to the trauma or something else they believe is in their control.

Trying to control a situation stops you from growing and adapting and keeps you stuck in a cycle of worry and anxiety. We must learn to stop believing the worst-case scenario and begin to see God in the middle of our situation. As Bill Johnson also says:

We must get our minds set on spiritual things because as long as we fill our minds with what's happening in the natural, we restrict our effectiveness. We may rise up now and then and score a victory with the gift of faith, but we won't have the continual influence of Kingdom transformation flowing through us.[4]

As Bill points out, we won't grow in our faith when we look at what's happening in the natural and use that as an excuse to believe the worst rather than seeing the situation with spiritual eyes. Having spiritual eyes means that you're looking beyond what you see in the natural, and instead, you look at the situation through the eyes of hope. You look with faith that God is with you and is able to work in your situation beyond your belief and beyond the natural.

When we look at things only in the natural, it can seem like we're doing it alone. We forget that we can cast our cares on God, and we instead try to calculate the fastest and easiest way out of the stressful situation we encounter. This leads to self-reliance and, ironically, more stress. After my thyroid removal and weight gain, I was sure I could get back to my pre-op body. And I thought I had the tools to get what I wanted—diet, exercise, I can do this! I put my body to work, and not only did I not see the results I wanted, but it left me more exhausted and stressed than before.

If we take over in manipulating and controlling the circumstances around us, it's then on us to see it through because we've removed God from the situation. If, instead, we offer it to God to take care of, we can rely on Him to see it through because it's His to handle. We have to get our hands off the situations we are trying to meddle in and let God take over because then He's responsible for the outcome, not us. After all, I don't know about you, but trying to run the world sounds pretty exhausting to me!

When we are stressed, most of us are not operating in our usual patterns and ways. We begin controlling the things around us that feel easiest to change, mostly the day-to-day things. You may want the house tidier than you normally would, or you may want the kids quieter than usual. Most of the time, we also have little to no extra space for people and their drama. We want everything small and tangible in life to go smoothly so that we feel even just a thimble-full of control—a tiny bit of ease and simplicity. Controlling the small things gives us a *false* sense of control. It may help you feel good in the short-term (that is, if it all goes how you'd like it to), but those feelings don't have longevity.

Inevitably, something at some point isn't going to go how you want it to, and you're back in the same position, dealing with the same feelings you were trying to avoid before. Remember that, because it's important: Feelings that are a result of controlling situations (sense of stability, euphoria of things going your way) are temporary and short-term, but dealing with the feelings associated with your problem (addressing the issue, addressing the worry) gives you long-term solutions and success.

COURSE CORRECTION

Sometimes, our minds are like pin-ball machines. If you look at a pin-ball machine, there's a vast area in which a tiny ball can navigate. However, the tiny ball is controlled by a very small lever. That lever has only one direction: up. Only a tiny lever and an even smaller ball are meant to control the entire outcome of the machine and the entire outcome of the game. You have no control over the direction of the ball. Your lever only flips one way every time. You may think you have control over the direction you want it to go, but your outcome is limited by the nature of the lever. It has only one direction and speed. There are so many factors out of your control that the ball will often end up ricocheting off something you didn't expect and landing in a completely different area than you intended. You have almost no physical control over the ball to go in a certain direction, because it has limited capability.

Much in the same way, when you're in the middle of a stressful time, your mind can be like the pin-ball that's bouncing and flailing around aimlessly. You try to get your mind back on track and get it to go in one direction, yet it seems all it takes is an unexpected thought popping up, and you're back on the pin-ball excursion, bouncing and flailing all over the place.

It takes real practice and intention to keep your mind

on the things that are above, as Paul writes in Colossians 3:2, "*Set your minds on things that are above, not on things that are on earth.*" We may know that truth, but how do we follow that through when we are in the middle of a stressful situation, a big decision, or a time of hurt, and our feelings and mind want to ping-pong around all over the place? How can you set your mind (and keep it set) on things above? How can you use your faith to believe in overcoming whatever you're facing, whether that be body image issues, health struggles, or difficult relationships? It seems those are the times when what you believe with your faith versus what you feel when your circumstances seem impossible can sometimes collide. That's why we tend to try and control the menial things when we feel like the big things are out of our control.

Ironically, control isn't as much in our grasp as we think it is, and striving for it creates a dependency on *ourselves* that isn't healthy as Christians. God is who we should be depending on, not ourselves. Can I control what happens to me? Can I control what someone else says or does, or thinks, or how they act? Absolutely not. But God continues to remind us to rely on *Him*.

Trust (lean on, rely on, and be confident) in the Lord and do good; so shall you dwell in the land and feed surely on His faithfulness, and truly you shall be fed. Delight yourself also in the Lord, and He will give you the desires and secret petitions of your heart. Commit your way to the Lord [roll and repose each care of your load on Him]; trust (lean on, rely on, and be confident) also in Him and He will bring it to pass. (Psalm 37:3–5 AMPC)

Lean on, trust in, and be confident in the Lord with all your heart and mind and do not rely on your own insight or understanding. In all your ways know, recognize, and acknowledge Him, and He will direct and make straight and plain your paths. (Proverbs 3:5–6 AMPC)

For I know the plans I have for you, declares the LORD, plans for welfare and not for evil, to give you a future and a hope. (Jeremiah 29:11)

We cannot rely on God and ourselves at the same time. I call that "part-time obedience." God gave us His Word—the Bible—to help guide us through life, and there are so many verses that teach us the importance of relying on God and trusting in Him instead of ourselves. Why did He talk about it so often in His Word? I think it's because He knows our human nature; He knows how easily we try to control our circumstances and outcomes. He had to remind us over and over in His Word because we need multiple reminders—we are, after all, a stubborn people. We get off course and must be reminded that we don't *need* to carry our burdens ourselves or try to solve our own problems.

We *can* choose to carry them if we want, though. He won't force us to give them to Him. He won't force surrender, but why would we not want to? Why would we reject freedom? Pride. Stubbornness. Ultimately, so many times, we do reject surrender and instead try to do it on our own. Like the Israelites, when, dear, fellow wanderers, will we learn?

When we step in and try to control our circumstances, we are, in essence, trying—but failing miserably—to play the role of God. If we are the ones in charge of our circumstances (doing it in the flesh), then *we* are also the ones responsible for seeing those circumstances through. In contrast, if we give our problems to God, we are allowing Him to take over, and *He* has the responsibility of seeing it through and working it out. Which one sounds better? In reality, He is always in control. But He can accomplish so much more in us when we recognize that and relinquish the tight grasp we have on life and our worries.

There is not a single verse in the Bible that instructs us to take matters into our own hands. Not one. Instead, in each and every instance in the Bible where God talks about what we should do when we are confronted with problems, we are told to pray about them.

*Do not be anxious about anything, but in everything **by prayer** and supplication with thanksgiving let your* *requests be made known to God. (Philippians 4:6–7, emphasis mine)*

Is anyone among you in trouble? **Let them pray.** *Is anyone happy? Let them sing songs of praise. (James 5:13 NIV, emphasis mine)*

He will listen to the **prayers** *of the destitute. He will not reject their pleas. (Psalm 102:17 NLT, emphasis mine)*

But in my distress I **cried out to the LORD;** *yes, I* **prayed** *to my God for help. He heard me from his sanctuary; my cry to him reached his ears. (Psalm 18:6 NLT, emphasis mine)*

He instructs us to give our worries to Him and let *Him* work it out. The battle is not ours, but God's (2 Chronicles 20:15). Do you actually and fully realize what a privilege that is? Ponder that for a moment.

We so easily forget this privilege. We get stuck trying to control situations, trying to orchestrate the outcome we desire, and by doing so, we bypass God and focus on what *we* can do to make it happen. Sometimes, we can even see faith as a hindrance to doing things our way. We ignore the sovereignty of God in our lives and try to take the reins ourselves. How many times have you planned out the rescue route that you believe God should take? How often have you given Him your well-laid-out plan and expected Him to follow it? Are you quick to tell Him the way He should do it? *Or do you desire to let God move your heart instead of you trying to move His hand?* Take a moment to answer that question honestly.

When we get to that place—which we all have at one time or another—we have, in essence, stopped surrendering. When that happens, we have two choices. One: We can recognize our desire to control and repent when the Holy Spirit reveals it to us, resulting in a good course correction. Or there's option two: We can reject small whispers from God and allow control to become part of our everyday rhetoric or practice. Once that happens, the course of action is beyond the realm of a course correction and turns into the realm of unlearning a deeply-rooted habit, which requires much more time, effort, and prayer to change.

Which scenario describes you? Do you just need a course correction in this area of control, or has it proceeded beyond a fumble here and there to something more deeply rooted and more habitual that needs change? Pause, put the book down, and do a self-check-in. Ask yourself how you're doing, and pray for the Holy Spirit's guidance now.

CONTINUAL SURRENDER

In some ways, I wish surrender was a one-and-done scenario, but it's not. I'd be popping a pair of rose-coloured lenses into your field of vision if I said something that isn't going to help you grow in truth. Surrender is a daily practice. We cannot just surrender once and think that's good enough or that it'll last us every day because, as my pastor often says, "We leak."[5] We do grow, and we do learn new things, and the Holy Spirit fills us up with knowledge and truth, but inevitably, sometimes those truths leak out. We need to continually fill our minds with the truth. We must keep practicing renewing our minds with God's Word—which is the truth. It's like trying to fill a sieve with water. We always need a steady stream of water (the truth) pouring into us. Just like forgiveness is the practice of *continually* forgiving, and repentance is the act of *continually* repenting of our sin similarly, surrender is the daily practice of *continually* surrendering.

It's like the manna that God gave the Israelites while they were wandering in the desert. It was only good for that day. If they tried to collect more than one day's worth, it went bad because God was teaching them to rely on Him for their *daily* needs and not rely on their resourcefulness. In the same way, we need to choose to *surrender to God daily* because surrender has a shelf life

—it won't last for weeks and weeks at a time, mostly due to our stubborn nature as humans and because, well, as we said, we leak.

Despite how little we enjoy it, we really do need circumstances that stretch us, because they humble us and help us recognize our need for God. They root out the pride that tells us we can do it on our own. Without that dose of humility, we are stubborn, and we get used to trying to do it on our own. God sometimes allows difficult circumstances to help us realize we can't do it on our own, and we need to surrender it all to Him.

God is so wise, though. He knows that we won't get it right all the time. We learn new things and apply them as much as we remember, but there are many times when that new knowledge escapes us, and we fall back into the old way of doing things. God knows this about us, and that's why He never gives up on us. He works on transforming that new information from head knowledge to heart revelation.

Life can be so busy, which is why the act of practicing these principles daily is so important for us. I would, however, argue that walking out these principles of spiritual discipline is becoming a lost practice. The Christian walk is a relationship first and foremost, but the Christian life also requires *practice*, not just *ideology*. Living victoriously doesn't come by accident; it's intentional, and it takes practice.

Have you ever accidentally gotten healthy? Have you ever fallen into good shape? Of course not! We don't get healthy by accident; we get healthy when we put effort into how we eat, exercise, and take care of our bodies and minds. In the same way, we don't get spiritually healthy by accident. It takes prayer, time, and reliance on the Holy Spirit to guide us. We can get easily distracted or bogged down by the world around us, so we need to continually connect with God through prayer and the Word as our daily course correction.

TRUSTING GOD'S SOVEREIGNTY

God promises to take care of us (1 Peter 5:7), yet we are often afraid to fully surrender it *all* to Him. Surrendering it all means we let go of suggesting our preferred route to God or our idea of the best way to go about it. I know I've fallen into that trap many times when I thought I knew better.

God knows what is best for us, and we either trust Him to take care of us like He says He will, or we don't—there isn't a middle ground. We aren't told to worry or figure out the plan; we are told to pray. Faith requires doing what the Word says in obedience rather than doubt. You can't rely on your feelings. You can't wait until you *feel* like trusting Him or *feel* like surrendering because that feeling may never come. Being victorious requires making good choices and not waiting for feelings to guide you.

It's true that there are many hard circumstances that we won't ever fully understand this side of heaven. I have had many questionable situations happen that I haven't had the answer to, and it can be hard at times. We want the answers because we believe they will make us feel better, and they may, but it's not our job to understand God's ways.

Ironically, there are many things in the world that I don't have to understand in order to use them: my TV, my car, microwaves, the internet, a cellphone, and many miracles of nature—honestly, the list is so large because there are many complexities I don't understand. I have no idea how they actually work, but I don't have to know that to use them. I use them because I *know* they work; the how or why doesn't matter.

The same can be true of faith. We don't always have to know the *why or how*, but thankfully, we know the *One* who knows, and we know the *Way*. He tells us in the Word what we should do. Pray. Trust. Hope. It's our choice whether we put our trust in Him without an explanation or not. He sometimes gives us the answer to the why, but other times, we are required to rely on our faith.

Control can affect any area of your life: external factors and how you feel about yourself, including what you see when you look in the mirror. Perhaps you've let your exterior become part of your identity or all of your identity. Maybe you're not enjoying today because of the way you look. You're so focused on what you want to be tomorrow that you're robbed of the joy of being at peace with how you look today. You're chasing after something that is elusive, unattainable, and out of reach. That "perfect" size you want to be, that "perfect" skin you want to have, that "perfect" ____; it doesn't exist. It *actually* doesn't exist—that's the truth. It doesn't exist because even if you were to get it, it wouldn't be enough. You'd reach that goal and then set a new one because the goalpost is always moving. You say, "No, once I reach ___, I will be happy." But you won't. How do I know that? Because the issue isn't with anything external; it's an internal issue. It's an idyllic image of what you think you should be rather than accepting who you are. The issue is your struggle to accept and love yourself and your body the way it is. The issue is with your heart and mind, not your body. The issue is you've let it become your identity.

Your body is going to change in a million ways over the course of your life; that's one thing you *can* count on. If you try to freeze-frame a moment in time and duplicate it for the rest of your life, you will find it impossible to maintain, and it will rob you of much joy, much contentment, and much peace. But what *is* possible is learning to love who God made you—heart, soul, and mind—and allowing God's love to flow in and through you. Once you start to see who God made you and stop trying to control what you see in the mirror, you will be set free. You'll be able to love what you see and accept that what you look like has no bearing on your worth. You'll be able to love what you see because you'll realize that what you see on the outside may be different than the beauty standards of the culture around you, but *what you see doesn't define who you are.* Getting those physical desires met won't fulfill you, despite feeling like they will. It's like trying to compare apples to atlases. It's not a fair comparison because they're completely different— different purposes, different materials, different uses. They are different in almost every way.

The culture around us has partnered with the lies of the enemy to make women everywhere believe that their worth is tied up in what they look like, based on what the culture says is acceptable. God's daughters have been robbed of their royalty, robbed of their peace and freedom, and robbed of their inheritance in Christ but robbed only in their minds. What they fail to realize is that those things are yours; they're still there—you just have to know and receive them. Thankfully, those promises haven't gone anywhere. You're still a daughter of the King, and you're still exactly who He says you are, but it's time to take back the truth and learn about your identity from your Father rather than from the culture.

CHAPTER THREE

Mirror, Mirror

"Mirror, mirror on the wall, who's the fairest of them all?" the queen cackled from her dark, stone castle. Day after day, her insatiable lust for outer beauty consumed her. In my mind's eye, I can picture her standing there, with her white, cartooned face and nose pointed in the air, staring at herself in the mirror. She had let her vanity steal not only her relationship with her step-daughter but her soul. She would ask the mirror daily to show her the most beautiful one in the land, and her soul was twisted and tortured every time the reflection of her step-daughter shone upon the mirror instead of her own. It mirrored the sickness in her own soul, longing and thirsting for a beauty that would never be. Her insatiable thirst for being the most beautiful was repeatedly denied, day after day, and it planted deep seeds of envy, jealousy, and bone-rotting anger toward her naturally beautiful step-daughter.

There was one thing she wanted more than anything. It ate away at her like a gangrenous sore, ravaging through flesh and marrow, eating away at the inner sinews of her very soul. Her seething jealousy and engrossing desire devoured her. She had but one aspiration, one desire, one obsession: to be beautiful. Although, not only to be beautiful but to be *the most* beautiful in the land.

Countless time was wasted on a fleeting dream that would never be realized. Endless sleepless nights were wasted. Relationships were ruined and poisoned by an unappeasable thirst that would never be quenched. She would stop at nothing, taking down anyone in her path—her own family, even her own soul—in pursuit of her vain desire. All her time, energy, and thoughts were devoured by her pursuit of beauty. It consumed her, haunting her inner being like a thick fog descending on a low valley and eventually leading to her tragic death.

Looking at this sad shell of a woman, I'm so thankful there's nothing resembling myself in her. Whew—dodged that bullet! It's a relief that I can't relate at all, isn't it? Right?

Or can I?

Although she took it to an extreme that I can't fathom, there are elements of her desire to be seen as beautiful that I, too, have striven for—we all have. Not unlike the queen, I have had moments of feeding that same desire for outer beauty, sometimes with external efforts but certainly with a deep striving in my soul that was misaligned with who I was created to be. The result? I turned into something less than my intended purpose, a vessel not for honourable use. In my soul, I've listened to the lie that who I am inside is just not enough, that who I am inside isn't accurately reflected on the outside, that who I am inside, in fact, doesn't measure up to what I should be. In believing those lies, I had given my appearance more value, thought, and time than it deserved. I had let it define me.

I've participated in the petty jealousy of women whose reflection appeared in the mirror instead of my own, straying down the ugly and pillaging path of comparison. I've sought my own selfish desires in order to calm an anxiousness in my soul that I thought could be quenched by seeing my image reflected back. Like the queen, I was relentless in my pursuit. Like the queen, I asked the same redundant question every single day, expecting a different answer: Am I enough? *If I just do **this**, I'll finally see myself as more beautiful. If I can just get to **this point**, I'll feel beautiful on the outside*—always asking the same question, always expecting a different answer, placing my value and worth in the wrong place, and hitching my wagon to the wrong star.

Pursuing the external desires of this world—no matter what they are: fame, financial success, beauty, social standing, or any such things—will not fill us in the way we think it will. We believe that if we pursue these external desires while loving Jesus, we are immune to the self-robbing effect they have on our lives. Or we believe that God will give us all the things we selfishly desire, because we think that's what is best for us. But my friend, being in relationship with Jesus isn't like rubbing the lamp, hoping for a genie to appear, ready to grant your three wishes. Often, He protects us from our selfish desires by *not* giving us what we ask for because it wouldn't be good for us. Trusting in God and His sovereignty means you trust that He knows what's best for you and what's not—trusting His will rather than yours.

Worth isn't an easy topic. We don't often talk about it around the dinner table, nor are we always real with ourselves about how it casts its shadow in our lives. I have had my own journey with the mirror—that shiny object reflecting an image that says nothing about who I am. That shiny object whose reflection holds so much value in our world today yet tells so many lies. It's nothing but a thin coat of aluminum and glass, yet the image it casts is the metric by which many women value themselves. The material that makes up a mirror is not expensive, yet the exorbitant cost to many women's mental health is very high. It's not the mirror that holds the value; it's the worth we believe we have or don't have based on the image reflected back to us. Image has been raised to a place of high prestige and unrealistic expectations.

IMAGES EVERYWHERE

Mirrors are everywhere. You'll find them in lobbies, elevators, bathrooms, homes, cars, and ceilings, as well as littered throughout the world of technology via phones and cameras. The real twist in the technology world is the addition of filters on cameras; the image reflected can be modified and tweaked, distorting any sense of reality. With the swipe of a finger, you can instantly alter your appearance, with many people opting for the flawless versions that plump your lips, enlarge your eyes, narrow your nose, and smooth your skin. One can even project this flawless version to the world without anyone knowing it, with just a simple tap of a button. Young girls and women of all ages are tricked into and trapped in a world with a warped sense of reality—one that's as fickle and as fragile as a house of cards. One slight move in either direction and the whole house—image, worth, value—could come crashing down, leaving them more empty than they were before.

The skewed version that women feel they need to live up to and project to the world has twisted reality, nearly the same way the pornography industry has twisted sex. We are living in a culture that has a warped sense of reality when it comes to things like sex and physical appearance, but it's portrayed and packaged up as if it's realistic or attainable—the ultimate goal.

We no longer have to wait and see the edited version of our images; we can edit our looks immediately—now, in real-time. How is this going to impact not only our current generation but more-so the young, impressionable, and upcoming generations? It is already having devastating effects on women's mental health, and now the younger generation is being sucked into this warped sense of reality at younger and younger ages, their brains not yet developed enough to take it all in and make sense of it. We are failing them if we refuse to acknowledge the importance of stopping this toxic pattern of perfectionism, and we are failing ourselves as well.

Truthfully, we are not immune at any age. Just because we are not adolescents anymore doesn't mean we are immune to the devastating effects of image management on our psyche.

Vanity can come in many forms, yet the form that's running rampant in our current culture is physical beauty. The image presented to girls and women of all ages is striving to look young and perfect—no flaws. The messaging for women in their twenties, thirties, forties, fifties, and onward is that we need to look young, much younger than we are. We are supposed to take our cues from the younger generation on how to emulate their youthful features on our faces. Yes, there are some isolated campaigns like Dove's, which are trying to change the messaging and push the ideology that women should embrace and accept themselves at any shape or size, but this is not the mainstream agenda or belief.

Not only are women told they need to continue to do all the things they are already responsible for, but there is also pressure today to be put together at all times. There is pressure to fit into the world with high-end, stylish clothing and a youthful complexion—not acknowledging the devastating effect it has on their bank account or emotional health.

Our culture preaches that you must also be sure to be slim and fit, or even one step further—sculpted. Keep in mind there's also the expectation that even when cleaning, exercising, or engaging in any other activity, you must look very put together. And that's just a fraction of the pressures placed upon women regarding physical appearance—let alone all the other areas we haven't discussed, such as having an immaculate and trendy home, perfectly behaved children, and a successful career to top it all off.

How, HOW—I ask you, with complete perplexity—are we supposed to live up to all that? Is it any wonder why mental health issues are at an all-time high in our society? You're either anxious because you are trying to do it all and suffocating under the pressure, or you're depressed because you realize you'll never stack up, so why bother trying? What is being portrayed to our daughters about how they need to function in the world? Is this the legacy we want to leave them? Do we want to exemplify that success is defined by appearance? Do we want to teach our girls to run around like mad-women trying to do it all?

I will admit that at times in the past, I have believed the lies, pursued attaining an impossible standard, and fallen into the trap. It was only by God's grace and plan of unexpected turns that He pulled me out of the miry, mucky clay and placed me on solid ground.

MIRROR, MIRROR, ON THE WALL

As I shared earlier, when I began my journey with my thyroid issues and gained a lot of weight, I was really hard on myself. I would look back at old photos of myself or stand in front of the mirror and feel like I was a fraud in my new body—an imposter. I felt like I didn't know who I was when my image was reflected back. I would look at myself in the mirror and not even recognize the person staring back at me. I was angry with my struggle. I was angry with my body. I was angry with my health. I was angry with the enemy. I was angry with how I felt—I wanted to be a hero of the faith, not a failure of it. How badly I had fallen into that pit of lies that told me I needed to look a certain way to be used by God or to be of value.

I had developed a belief that I didn't realize I held until the Holy Spirit revealed the truth to me much later on in my journey. I thought that acceptance meant fitting in on the outside. I believed that people were my friends because of how I looked. I believed that in our superficial culture, in order to fit in and be accepted, one had to look a certain way. But that's the problem with a lie—it isn't true, but it can feel true. And that's the messaging the enemy had been telling me since I was a young child—reinforced by the culture, of course.

The problem, I learned, with believing that my friendships were based on some sort of performance, was that it would need to be a continual cycle of performance. Believing that lie meant that I would have to continue to maintain that performance in order to keep people as friends. And I was able to keep up the performance . . . until my thyroid journey. At that point, I couldn't perform anymore, no matter how much I tried—the weight piled on whether I wanted it to or not. And that's when my proverbial house of cards came crashing down. I had to recognize the lie and learn the truth about how others saw me and how I saw myself. I had to allow God to show me that others' love for me wasn't based on what I could do for them or who I could pretend to be but that I could receive their love for me, just as I was. And that required a lot of unlearning.

The enemy put me through so much torment, trying to make me believe I needed to live up to the world's standard of beauty to be accepted. It only amplified my feelings of failure. I was looking in all the wrong places to feel normal, accepted—special. I was focusing on all the wrong things—all the external things. The enemy knows that if he can take your eyes off Jesus (the solution) and put them on your problems, he can begin to plant doubts about who you are.

I thought that perhaps if I found just the right combination of factors that could bring happiness, then I could restore the joy that the enemy had stolen from me. But *you cannot fix an internal issue with external solutions*. You cannot fix an enemy problem with a worldly solution—God is the only solution. The enemy may try to win the battle, but the war is the Lord's.

While dealing with all the physical changes taking place, I was also dealing with emotional changes at the same time. Hormonal fluctuations didn't help. World-wide lockdown didn't help. Ironically, I would never fault anyone else for weight gain, yet somehow, I was incredibly hard on myself, and part of the path to healing and wholeness has been a lot of forgiveness—for myself.

At the beginning of that journey, I felt like God had somehow let me down, and just like Jacob, I refused to stop wrestling until I got my miracle (see Genesis 32). I didn't care if it meant I would walk with a limp for the rest of my days; I wanted a miracle. At that time, a miracle to me meant returning to my old self, the size I used to be. I wasn't asking God to help me grow where I was or asking

Him how He was using the situation for my good; I was narrow-minded and wanted Him to make things go back to the way they were. I, like the Israelites, wanted to go back to the slavery in Egypt rather than the Promised Land of freedom. I didn't care that it meant slavery; I just wanted what I used to have. I had stopped looking to God as the solution and looked at my weight as a burden rather than part of my journey to freedom. And my friend, I can say now that this journey has been a gift—but more about that later.

EGYPT MENTALITY

For years, when I read Exodus 14, I could not, for the life of me, understand the Israelites and their desire to return to slavery in Egypt when they were pressed by Pharaoh and his army at the Red Sea (one time among many when they complained about their freedom). For years, it made *no* sense to me.

> *When the Israelites saw the king coming with his army, they were frightened and begged the LORD for help. They also complained to Moses, "Wasn't there enough room in Egypt to bury us? Is that why you brought us out here to die in the desert? Why did you bring us out of Egypt anyway?* ***While we were there, didn't we tell you to leave us alone? We'd rather be slaves in Egypt than die in this desert!****"* (Exodus 14:10–12 CEV, emphasis mine)

It seemed incredibly short-sighted to me to want to go back to long hours, pain, no pay, whippings, and beatings when, instead, they could have freedom from slavery in an abundant and plentiful land. Why would anyone want the former over the latter?

I often asked myself, "Did they hear themselves? Why would they want to go back to slavery rather than follow Moses to the Promised Land?" Many times, I rolled my eyes at their stupidity. Wasn't freedom the clear choice? But one day, God opened my eyes, and I got it.

Egypt did mean slavery for them, but Egypt was also familiar. It was all they'd known. It was what they were raised in; it was part of their mindset. They were treated terribly by the Egyptians, but they hadn't yet tasted what freedom was—they had no concept of what it could be. Egypt was torture, but Egypt was what they knew.

The Promised Land, on the other hand, was freedom, but they didn't know what freedom felt like, looked like, and tasted like. They had no idea what to expect. The Promised Land was unfamiliar, unknown. Because they didn't know what freedom could be and facing the unknown felt uncomfortable, they believed it was better to return to slavery—at least it was familiar. I know it seems crazy, but the logic stands—we do the same thing!

Think about a time when you went back to an old habit or pattern that wasn't good for you because it was more comfortable than trying something new or stepping into discipline, and so you reverted back to your old slave lifestyle. Sounding familiar? I know, I know, it was a light bulb moment for me, too.

I wonder how many times we settle for the slavery of Egypt over the freedom of the Promised Land. I wonder how often we trade slavery for freedom because we don't know what freedom really feels like. I wonder how often we beg God to return us to our Egypt, to our comfort, to what we know, to our former patterns, to the old way of life, because we are afraid of the unfamiliar, the unknown. If we trusted God's goodness for us, wouldn't we trust that even the unknown of God's plan is better than the familiar of ours? It makes me wonder if we don't know what true freedom feels like. Maybe we don't fully know if it's as good as He says—if *He's* as good as He says. That's a tough question to ponder but one that begs a look.

Sadly, because we don't know what we are missing out on or haven't fully trusted God's good plan, we cling to our slavery in Egypt. We are afraid of the unknown, the other side. Walking forward into freedom can be more uncomfortable than turning to the bondage left behind if we haven't tasted the goodness of God. But before we can set foot in the Promised Land, we have to take that first step of faith toward our good God. We have to take our first step of faith onto the ocean bed and cross over to the other side. We need to trust God's character and His goodness rather than believe that what we had was "fine." If we don't, we will miss out on what is coming, which is far, far better.

All along the Israelites' journey, God showed up for them time and time again. He performed miracles, He led them, He provided for them, and yet, they struggled to embrace the new way of life He had planned for them. They continued to revert back to their slave mindsets. They lived in the bondage of their minds, never understanding the freedom they could receive if they just trusted and followed God. The same is true for you. You won't ever flourish in the Promised Land if you keep your mind on Egypt, on the past, and on the lies you've believed. Those mindsets need to be cast off, washed in the waters of faith.

God gave the Israelites many, many opportunities to change their Egypt mindset, yet they struggled to let it go. And so He had to start fresh with a new generation of Israelites who were not born into slavery but were birthed into freedom.

I clung to the Egypt of my closet, holding onto old clothes that used to fit, telling myself, *I'll get there one day*—the lie that feels so true. I kept telling myself I would be happy when I "got there," as if it meant that someday I would actually arrive at a destination. It didn't matter that being a slave to a smaller size was short-sighted and cruel;

it was comfortable.

I refused to give up, even though I could feel the clothes digging into my skin, too small for my new body —the constant pinching a present reminder of the size I once was.

I lived with an Egypt mindset. What I was dealing with and how I was going about it in my thoughts wasn't good for my mind, emotions, self-image, or my relationship with God. After all, He created me; He loved me so deeply, and here I was, treating His creation like a cracked clay pot, not fit for honourable use.

I was in the Word daily, but I wasn't studying in the areas I was weak in. I wasn't addressing the hidden issues below the surface. I didn't remind myself what God's Word said about me as His child, because I didn't really know. I was letting the reflection in the mirror define what I thought about myself.

I had been a Christian my entire life, and a dedicated one at that, yet I had never really learned about my true identity, my inheritance, or how God saw me. I was completely weak in my understanding of my identity in Christ, so when the enemy spoke lies to me, I easily fell for his tricks because his lies are often sneaky.

God was always speaking the truth to me; I just had to listen to His whisper rather than the lies, which are often loud. I had to become strong and well-versed in the truth so I could be strong and equipped to recognize the lies.

Sometimes, I would let my feelings and emotions (which are dependent on circumstances) take the lead rather than the truth of God's Word, which is not fleeting.

But in that season, when I longed desperately for the mirror to reflect something familiar, God began to speak to me. He quieted the lies around me and let His voice come through loud and clear. Through His Word, I learned about who I am, my value, my worth, and most of all, my identity in Christ. Once you know who you are in Christ, it changes everything. It doesn't mean you don't ever struggle or have moments when you need to remind yourself of the truth, but those moments are more few and far between than they used to be.

I'm not saying my transformation was instant. Like the Israelites, I walked a journey where God put miracle after miracle in my path. Like the Israelites, He took me the long way around rather than the shorter route because I needed to know Him more. He kept showing up, and eventually, I learned to look to Him rather than the external markers of beauty and worth. I can honestly say I don't struggle with the mirror the way I used to. I seek the approval of others less than I ever have before. I rarely wander down the road of comparison anymore, and if I do, I catch myself quickly. God has redeemed my Egypt and traded it for the Promised Land, but it was a wilderness journey that needed to take place—a journey of humility and walking closely with the Lord.

This journey is why you're holding this book today. Once God had done this work in me, I couldn't help but share this message of hope. If you struggle with seeing your value, you will be easily assaulted by any critique that comes your way. As Alexander Hamilton said, "Those who stand for nothing fall for anything."[6] We need to know who we are, but more importantly, who we are in Christ—how God sees us. If you can stand confident in where your value comes from, that confidence will help you surrender the hardness in your heart to God, so that He can give you a soft heart in exchange: *"And I will give you a new heart, and I will put a new spirit in you. I will take out your stony, stubborn heart and give you a tender, responsive heart"* (Ezekiel 36:26 NLT).

I've finally stepped out of hiding and allowed others to see who God made me. Not only my personality and the gifts He's given me—I've always been fairly authentic with that—but I've finally embraced who He made me: spirit, soul, and *body*. I've stopped trying to be something I'm not. I've stopped trying to hide my flaws, and instead, I've embraced them as part of my story. I've begun to see myself the way God sees me: beautiful in His sight. I don't measure myself by the measuring-stick of the culture; I measure myself by who Jesus says I am and who He's made me to be, inside and out.

The reflection that once held me back, that made me hide, believing I was less than everyone else, has no power over me anymore. That mirror holds no truth—I now walk in freedom because of my true identity.

BODY, MIND, AND SPIRIT

It seems holier, somehow, to reject our humanness—holier to try and convince ourselves that the things that are part of being human shouldn't affect us. We contemplate the idea that if we could just attain more closeness with God, then the rest would just fade away—our human desires would simply cease to exist. We try to convince ourselves that the fine lines and round curves somehow shouldn't matter in comparison to Jesus or that holiness means rejecting beauty and letting one's self go. We may be tempted to rid ourselves of all worldly attributes and embody a "John the Baptist-like" persona. We think holiness means stripping one's self of all awareness of one's physical self—to feel beautiful would be a betrayal of religion, of sanctification, of closeness with our Creator. This dichotomy hits deep; it embodies the struggle.

But there's a problem with it—we *are* human, body, mind, and spirit.

It's true that He is enough and even more than we could ever need. He is sufficient for everything we need and desire. But it's also true that we live in a mortal body —we are, indeed, human. We have desires and needs that are both physical and emotional. When Jesus was on the earth, fully man and fully God, He still had to feed His body—He didn't just spiritualize His need for food, pray, and believe He was full. No, He had to physically eat food because He recognized the reality of His humanness.

We can pursue a deeper relationship with God without ignoring who we are as humans. After all, He created us as humans. If He wanted us to be angels or spiritual creatures, He would have created us that way, but He didn't—He created us just as He wanted us, made in *His* image.

We can get stuck believing we have to choose one side, one camp, one ultimatum. But it's not as though we have to choose one side or the other: holiness or humanness—*it's yes to both*. We don't need to put ourselves or God in a box and say, "To be holy is to deny who God made me." That's not right; that's not accepting who He made us to be. Instead, we must echo, "To be who God made me is to embrace who I am in my humanness and see my need for Him—to earnestly seek to be more like Him." *It's yes to both*—not either/or.

Oftentimes, we feel we have to choose. We believe that if we give into something that is part of our humanness, we are rejecting godliness, and there are times when that's true. Gluttony is choosing the love of food over God. Sexual sin is choosing sexual gratification over God. Obsession with beauty is choosing vanity over God. Anything that's out of balance or against God's nature is giving into the desires of the flesh, which can get between us and God. Yes, we must die to our carnal desires that aren't glorifying to God, but you shouldn't reject who God made you—uniquely and individually—because you think you're not holy enough. The truth is, you're not. I'm not. None of us will ever be holy enough, but that's why we so desperately need a Saviour.

The flip side is we cannot deny that we were created as humans in *God's* image (Genesis 1:26–27). If that humanness (our desires, nature, etc.) is submitted to God and in balance, it is good. Humanity fell, and sin entered the world, but that's why God sent His Son to save us. Holiness is a life-long ambition, and we can't expect to be perfect while here on earth, but we can see our need for a Saviour.

God did not make us strictly spiritual beings. He gave us wants, desires, and emotions. He gave us human bodies that need to eat to live. He gave us human bodies that need sleep and rest, oxygen and water. Our bodies have needs that we cannot ignore by spiritualizing them. What good would it do to just believe we could receive water spiritually without actually drinking it? What good would it do to simply believe that you could get in shape without ever exercising? That would be absolute foolishness.

God gave us human emotions that thrive on connection with others. He gave us human emotions that seek closeness with each other and with Him. Jesus embraced His godliness, but He also embraced His humanity. He knew that He was both divine and human. He wept because He was human. He prayed because He was spiritual. He ate because He was human. He did God's will because He was spiritual. He didn't have to choose between the two. *It's yes—to both.*

God doesn't say we should denigrate ourselves; He said that He made us beautiful in His sight. Now, has the culture distorted what that looks like? Absolutely. Has it become unbalanced? Yes. Does that mean we should reject anything to do with beauty simply because the culture got it wrong? No. Just because the culture has distorted it doesn't mean we need to throw it all away. The world has distorted many things that God made, but that doesn't mean we have to reject all those things in their natural form.

The world has distorted sex, for example, and because of that, there is a massive, thriving pornography industry. Pornography and all of its effects are evil. It has ruined more relationships, marriages, and people's mental health than can be counted. It is completely out of line with what God created when He designed sex. Sex was purposed for intimacy in a marriage between a husband and his wife. Does that mean what God made was wrong because the world has distorted it? Absolutely not. What God made is still good, it is still right, and it is still beautiful when used as He designed it. The world has made a distorted and perverse version of what God initially intended and created for good. What was designed as good can become evil when put in the wrong hands.

> *Woe to those who call evil good*
> *and good evil,*
> *who put darkness for light*
> *and light for darkness,*
> *who put bitter for sweet*
> *and sweet for bitter!*
> *Isaiah 5:20*

Satan uses circumstances to try to force us into extreme measures because He knows it will eventually cause things to get out of balance. Out-of-balance individuals are unhappy individuals because we were designed with balance and alignment in mind. An out-of-balance mindset causes us to focus on ourselves—what we can or can't do in our strength, rather than relying on God.

Ephesians 2:10 says, "*We are his workmanship, created in Christ Jesus for good works, which God prepared beforehand, that we should walk in them.*" Not only did He say He made us in His image, but He worked hard to make sure the earth He made for us was good and that it pleased Him.

God talks throughout the Bible about beauty. He made you precious in His sight (Isaiah 43:4), and that's good;

however, lusting after beauty is not. Making it an idol is not. Letting physical beauty come between you and God is not good. But when you feel confident in who God made you to be, inwardly as well as outwardly, and embrace who you are and the skin that clothes you, that is a celebration of God and His handiwork. We aren't meant to be full of ourselves or in love with ourselves, but neither are we meant to denigrate ourselves because in doing so, we are saying that what God made isn't good. We need to find balance in knowing who we are in Christ, which gives us a right view of our relationship with God.

FINDING BALANCE IN BEAUTY

Matthew 26:41 tells us, *"The spirit is willing, but the flesh is weak"* (NIV). If you are just starting out on this journey toward balance, it will probably take time for you to walk out what you learn. It did for me. You're reprogramming your mind to believe the truth rather than lies, which takes time and practice. You're creating new pathways and patterns in your mind that remind you of the truth instead of the lies. It likely won't happen overnight, although God can absolutely, miraculously step in and do it any way He chooses, but most of the time, it takes time, prayer, and practice.

Earlier, I told you that going through what I did was the gift I didn't know I needed. What I meant by that is that hardships are never fun—let's just make that clear. But they're often the means by which God is able to work out maturity and growth in us. Had I not come face to face with my insecurity, I would not have gone through the hard (but healing) work of discovering my true identity, and I would have been robbed of the joy of finding my worth and value in my loving Saviour. My greatest challenge ended up being my greatest victory.

Oftentimes, we think healing is a one-time miracle (and it can be sometimes), but more often than not, it takes time. As long as we are alive, we are thinking, and as long as we are thinking, the enemy will always try to get a foothold in our mind, so we need to do what Scripture says and: *"Be sober-minded; be watchful"* and *"run with endurance the race that is set before us"* (1 Peter 5:8; Hebrews 12:1).

Never once will God leave you alone while you're muddling through the muck. He will lovingly pour out His grace. He did it for me, and He will do it for you, too!

How do you learn to love who God made you? Prayer, reading God's Word, and time. See what He says about you. See what He promises you. See who *He* is, His character. Give God time to work your mess out as you pray and study Scripture. Oftentimes, it's a battle in our minds more than anything else. Our mind is where God speaks the truth, but it's also the place the enemy plants lies—it's the battlefield.[7] We need to learn our identity in Christ in order to begin replacing the lies with the truth.

Changing a pattern of thinking will take time, but you can get there if you stay committed and continue to pray. *"So let's not get tired of doing what is good. At just the right time we will reap a harvest of blessing if we don't give up"* (Galatians 6:9 NLT).

That's a promise from God to you, and it's one that's been so encouraging to me to keep trusting God to renew my mind. Sometimes, the revelation comes in dribs and drabs, and other times, God rushes in like a tidal wave and gives you such a deep revelation that it completely changes your life in an instant.

A moment when God came in like a tidal wave and instantly changed my heart was one night about a year ago. God had been working on my heart, walking me through some of the past hurts that I'd experienced that contributed to me feeling unworthy and was helping me heal from those wounds.

One night, I was awoken out of sleep, which is pretty rare for me. I said a quick prayer and asked God to show me if there was something I needed to know. I waited a moment and didn't hear anything, so I went back to sleep.

At 3:15 a.m. I was awoken again, but this time because of a dream I had just dreamt. This dream had profound meaning to me, relating to a traumatic experience from the past, and when I woke up, God immediately gave me the interpretation. God used the dream to show me this trauma was lingering from when I was *very* young, from being abused as a young child by someone outside our family—trauma that I thought had no effect on me. God revealed to me how it was showing up in my behaviour and ways of thinking and even core beliefs I had carried with me since I was young. It affected how I saw God as my Father/Protector because I had felt so unprotected due to the abuse, and it also affected how I behaved in relationships. He began to show me the layers that I had hidden behind to protect myself from feeling pain—at least, I *thought* I needed to protect myself as no one else was going to do it for me. He showed me I had become self-protecting rather than allowing Him to be my Protector.

As God showed me how my story connected with a lifetime of striving for acceptance and worth, things began to fall into place. It was like a movie reel playing in my head; scenario after scenario began to make sense. Certain challenging relationships began to click. Understanding why I react in certain ways to situations began to click. Situation after situation, emotion after emotion, click after click after click, my life's story began to make so much sense. I realized that my striving for worth and value came from feeling that I had none. It came from feeling like I wasn't worthy of protection because when you think about it, things or people that are of value are fiercely protected. *Protection denotes value.* Protection also denotes love. It wasn't anyone's fault that I wasn't protected, but trauma doesn't understand things logically. Added to that, we have an enemy who loves to strip away our true identity and our true value by telling us lies.

Not receiving that protection drastically affected how I received my Heavenly Father's love, but also how I received the love of those around me. I strived for acceptance in ways that weren't healthy, controlling my looks (staying thin enough) because I thought people were my friends based on how I looked. I strived for attention from boys as a teen, hoping someone would make me feel of value, and I strived to be perfect to everyone around me in how I conducted myself, afraid that they'd somehow see the real me, the imperfect me, the *damaged* me, and inevitably realize there was nothing of value there.

The trauma and abuse that I suffered at such a young age had been an open door for the enemy to lie to me for many, many years. He tried to convince me (and did a pretty good job because I believed it), telling me just how unworthy I was and that I was damaged goods. That script played in my head for most of my life—that I would forever be "damaged goods."

But thank God for His truth!

I laid there in my bed, overwhelmed (in a good way) and in awe of what God had shown me, but also overwhelmed with such joy because it was as if a truckload of bricks had been taken off my shoulders. He showed me all the ways I had sought to fill that hole, all the striving I had acted out for most of my life. Scene after scene played through my mind, and with each one, He showed me where He was in it all. He showed me the inner strength that He had put inside of me. He showed me how His strength helped me through it, that by God's grace, I had never turned to alcohol or drugs (as so many who come from abuse do), but instead, He gave me the grace to turn to Him in my pain. He was my rescue. He was there all along, helping me get through it and keeping me on the narrow path despite life's circumstances. He showed me the truth about it all, and in doing so, He began a deep, healing work in my heart in that very moment. I laid there in my bed at 3:30 in the morning, deeply impacted, tears streaming down my face; not tears of sadness, but tears of release.

Then, suddenly, there came a great moment of impact. His tidal wave of mercy was about to sweep in, change me, and set me free. In my mind's eye, I immediately saw myself standing in the sky, among the clouds, and in front of me was a wall of a dozen closed windows. There was a *huge* gust of wind that came from behind me, and the wall of windows burst open. In that very instant, an immense feeling of being *completely set free* washed through my entire body, from the top of my head to the tip of my toes. I have never felt so light, so weightless, or *so seen* before in my entire life.

Freedom filled my heart, spirit, and mind like I've never experienced—an absolute flood. There was freedom because God's presence had come. His presence rested on me like a cloud; I didn't want it to ever end. In my desire to draw near to Him by walking out this journey and learning to know my identity in Him, *He* drew near to me. He had come to set me free, like it says in 2 Corinthians 3:17, "*Where the Spirit of the Lord is, there is freedom*" (NIV). His presence, there with me in that room, was enough to completely change me. Just one touch of the hem of His garment, and I was utterly undone. I arose from the ashes brand new. What I experienced that night and in that moment is hard to adequately express in words other than to say it was like an old dusty attic that had been aired out. The windows flung open, and fresh air flew through the space and aired out everything that was dark, dusty, and dingy. In the very same way, freedom swept through my entire being, and my friend, it has forever changed me. Something changed in that moment —something that's stayed with me ever since.

The chains were broken off of me, and I was free. I felt God's love wash over me, and I was so full of joy for the gentle way in which He chose to love me. There was no way I could have figured it out on my own or experienced that kind of freedom and love from a cerebral place—it needed to be a touch from Him. God knew the perfect timing; He knew when I was ready to receive His healing love. That's why I say that oftentimes it doesn't happen that way, but sometimes, just sometimes, it does.

Unacknowledged trauma doesn't go away; it just lies dormant behind coping mechanisms, but once you face it, you can deal with it and then heal from it. Sometimes, that's through the work of a counsellor or a friend, but sometimes, it's through the work of one touch by the hand of God.

God gave me a gift. Sometimes, healing is a process, but other times, it's an immediate restoration. In this instance, it was instantaneous.

I hear woman after woman tell me about the pain they feel, struggling to feel worthy in their skin. I've had countless conversations with women over the years who have shared the deep, heart-wrenching things they struggle with in relation to their physical appearance.

It breaks my heart to see women tear themselves down regarding their bodies, and it's all too common in this world that objectifies women. They tear themselves down for all kinds of reasons, but often, it's because of past hurts and wounds that haven't healed. We all carry scars from some situation or another that cast its net of pain on us, whether it's an insecurity about looks because they were teased about it as a child or how they feel about themselves after having kids or aging.

Sometimes, women are insecure about their bodies even though they completely fit the mold relating to the world's beauty standards. Every woman I've ever talked to about body image will share one or two or more things that they don't like about their bodies, something they wish they could change. Some just flippantly comment on what they don't like, but don't intend on doing anything about it, while others go to great lengths to try and "fix" what they think needs fixing through various means.

Changing who you are on the outside doesn't make you less holy, but it means there's probably still some lingering brokenness or insecurity. There may be roots to some lies that need to be pulled out, possibly a result of some traumas from the past. We can't run from our traumas. They are open wounds that will never heal unless they're dealt with. That's what I discovered when God stepped in to heal every broken wound that stemmed from my past.

Dear friend, I want you to know something: God has *such good plans* for you. He has your path to freedom mapped out if you walk with Him and trust Him. Look to Him, not the mirror. Look to what He says about you and not the reflection you see in the mirror. If you're going to reflect something, let it be the character of Christ.

Don't worry about rushing the process. Don't worry about getting it all right. Don't worry about figuring it all out by yourself because, as much as you can try, you'll never know yourself the way God knows you. His intimate knowledge of you goes beyond comprehension and into the deepest, most hidden parts of you. We are all clay, and we can be moldable and movable when we allow Him to step in and remold us, even if it means starting all over again. Pray and seek the Lord for His restoration because one touch from Him will change your life.

CHAPTER FOUR

Who Told You That?

In the story *The Wizard of Oz,* Dorothy, a sweet young girl, was lost in a strange land and couldn't find her way home. She encountered three pivotal characters along her journey who agreed to try and help her get home. They all told her that the only man who could help her was a great and powerful wizard, the Wizard of Oz. His reputation in the land was one of much power and goodness. They told her if she could just get there to see him, the wizard would surely help her get back home, which she so desperately wanted.

Dorothy and her three friends travelled many miles to get to the Emerald City, seeking to meet the illustrious and powerful Wizard of Oz. They finally arrived after much hardship and trouble, and she was excited at the prospect of finally getting to go home.

When Dorothy and her three friends finally entered the long hallway leading to the wizard, they were scared. The room was dark and thick with fog, and there were pillars of fire around them. The wizard called them forward in a booming voice. As they walked down the long, dark hallway and into the great room, they saw an image of the wizard's face on a screen with fire burning all around him.

Each time they asked him a question, his anger rose, as did the sound of his voice and the flames of fire. He had, indeed, created a smoke-screen of deity and power to illicit fear so no one would question him or his power.

Dorothy made her request to the wizard to help her get home, and to her great surprise, he told her he wouldn't help her get home, and he turned Dorothy and her friends away. But Dorothy mustered up enough courage to ask again, pleading with him. He became angry with her, yelling even louder, with more smoke and fire billowing into the room in an attempt to scare them away. But Dorothy and her friends were determined and tenacious, and they continued to plead and beg the great wizard.

While they were trying to reason with the wizard, Dorothy noticed her dog Toto tugging at a closed curtain over to the side. As Toto tugged at the curtain, it began to open, and Dorothy saw that there was a man behind the curtain. He was yelling into a microphone and pressing all kinds of buttons and knobs. The man turned around and noticed that he had been exposed by the open curtain, so he rushed to quickly close it and conceal himself. He yelled into the microphone, "Pay no attention to the man behind the curtain!!"

At first, Dorothy wasn't sure what was going on or who the man behind the curtain was, but her curiosity propelled her to investigate further. She took a step closer.

The wizard, on the other hand, was terrified. He didn't want to be exposed as a fraud. He had worked so hard to conceal himself in obscurity and to stay trapped in his tiny pit of power—at least, his *illusion* of power. "Oh dear," he cried out as he fumbled to close the curtain that no longer provided shelter from his lies. He was distraught and caught off-guard as he tried to continue in character, to continue the charade, pretending to be the great and powerful Wizard of Oz. He clumsily fumbled with the silk curtain, trying to close it, while again yelling into the microphone, "Pay no attention to the man behind the curtain!" He was still trying to convince them that their eyes were deceiving them—that they were not seeing what they knew they were seeing.

"Pay no attention to the man behind the curtain!!" he said again, this time yelling into his booming microphone, flashing the lights and fire into the great room, pressing every button and knob on his light and smoke circuit board. He hoped his antics would distract them and fool them into believing he was the great and powerful Wizard of Oz, not just a simple man behind a curtain. He figured that if perhaps *he told them the lie enough times, they would believe it*. Maybe they would believe his lies rather than what they saw with their eyes. Maybe he could convince them of the lie *just enough* to question the truth —you know, plant just a little doubt. Maybe if he kept up the charade, they wouldn't notice that he wasn't a powerful wizard, burning in anger with smoke and fire, but a simple man who used lighting and showmanship tactics to project himself as a powerful, supernatural being. Maybe if he could conceal his true identity a little longer, they would just believe that he was who he projected himself to be.

Pay no attention to the man behind the curtain.

But the truth, eventually, *always* comes out.

Dorothy enters the tiny booth and sees all the dials, buttons, microphone, and other tricks the man has been using to confuse everyone who met him into believing he was a supernatural wizard. She quickly realizes he has been fooling her and her friends, not to mention the entire city. All it took was a brief moment of exposure, and his entire facade came crumbling down around him. It took him years to create his persona, but only one gust of wind to take it all down.

FALSE IMAGES

I spent many years of my life struggling to accept who I was. At times, I was ashamed of things from my past that held me captive. Other times, I looked at what I didn't have instead of what I did, or I compared myself to others, and I often felt I came up short. So often, I focused on *what I wasn't* rather than *who I was*.

A mindset like that is fraught with disappointment, jealousy, and tears. It created habits and routines in me that, over time, became deeply-formed ruts that I felt I could not climb out of. I wasn't at all aware of the thin tread-lines that were forming in the dirt, but the ruts that started out as shallow tracks eventually became deep trenches. Subtle changes here and there slowly emerged from the lies of the culture around me, and they had, over time, quietly embedded themselves in my mind.

I couldn't accept my flaws, so I wondered how anyone else could. I hid behind a thin veil of obscurity, a veil that surrounded me, a smoke-screen.

We get comfortable behind our curtains, don't we? We figure if we can just pretend, if we can just keep up the charade, if we can just present a version of ourselves that's acceptable to the world, we might get by just enough to convince people we are who we project to be.

However, living behind the curtain is a lonely life. Very few, if any, get to know the real you. Very few, if any, are able to see the true person behind the facade. Very few, if any, get to see all the beauty you have to offer. Worst of all, you miss out on real, true, authentic relationships. True relationships are always *just slightly* out of reach, slightly beyond the curtain. Sadly, you are robbing the world of all you have to offer, all that God's made you to be.

See, if you stay hidden behind the veil of fabric, you don't have to show who you are. You don't have to face judgment from others, and you don't have to worry about the real you being rejected—only the imitation you. From behind the protection of the curtain, you can make yourself into anyone you want to be, but behind the curtain, life is unpredictable. One slight gust of wind could blow the curtain sideways, just enough for someone to catch a glimpse, just enough for someone to peer behind the curtain and see the real you.

The Wizard of Oz hid himself behind a curtain because he didn't want people to know who he really was. He projected an image of power and prestige, but *only he* knew that he was neither of those things. He hid behind a curtain, in the dark, because he didn't want people to see who he really was.

Pay no attention to the man behind the curtain.

Even we are not immune to trying to project something inauthentic. Much like the wizard, we can project a version of ourselves that we want others to see and believe about who we are. You may mask yourself behind a perfectly curated social media profile, posting the highlight reels of your life in order to project a version of yourself that you want others to believe. Or, maybe, you strive to project a physical image of yourself, mimicking the flawless women on magazine covers, striving to meet the world's unrealistic standards, hoping it'll distract everyone from seeing the insecurity that's lurking behind the plastic mask.

Whatever your mask, your facade, or your bubble, they will all eventually fail. Eventually, the mask will fall. Eventually, the facade will come crashing down. Eventually, the bubble will pop because no matter how much you try to project a version of yourself to the world or those around you, the truth always comes out.

Pay no attention to the man behind the curtain.

Hiding behind a mask all the time is an empty place. Always playing the part is exhausting, anxiety-provoking, stressful, misleading, and unfulfilling. And it's not as if you picked up your mask because you were trying to deceive anyone; often, we pick up our masks as a way of coping and surviving the things we don't want to face, or even, at times, the things we don't realize we are struggling with.

You don't need to feel ashamed if you recognize that you've been wearing a mask or two, but it's good that you see it now because it allows you to take a moment to realize you can lower the mask, put it aside, and let the

Holy Spirit step in to work with you.

At different times in my life, I have hidden behind the curtain. The curtain of fear, the curtain of doubt, the curtain of insecurity. Sometimes, it felt easier in the moment to pretend to have it all together than to be honest and vulnerable. Yes, I would confess my struggles to God, but I was too ashamed to openly confess them to anyone else. I didn't want to admit that I felt inept, incapable, less-than—damaged goods, much of it stemming from the abuse I underwent as a child. I had shut myself into a world of curtains and doors, unable to find my way out. I became accustomed to the plastic smile. When asked how I was doing, without hesitation, I easily touted off the automatic response that I was good.

NOT GOOD ENOUGH?

Why do we struggle so often with these issues as women? Where did it all start? A very long time ago, in a garden with a lie and a serpent. It's the oldest lie of all time, spoken from the mouth of a slippery, sinister serpent to an innocent Eve in the Garden of Eden: *"You are not enough."*

Have you heard that lie before? "You are not enough." You should be "more beautiful." "More thin." "More youthful." "More smart." "More perfect." More, more, more, because you are: *Just. Not. Enough.*

Much like the wizard, the enemy puts on a facade, too. He hides behind showy tactics and smoke-and-mirrors power. He masquerades himself as someone he is not. He tries to convince you of the lies, even if the truth is in plain sight. He tries to convince you to doubt the truth—even if just a little. He sits in his pit of deception, hidden behind the curtain, afraid of exposure, afraid he'll be found out for the liar he is.

Honestly, Eve always gets a bad rap in the Bible. She is blamed throughout history for the choice she made. Yes, she did make a decision that changed the course of history. She disobeyed God. But is she the only one who's ever been deceived by the enemy? The only one who's ever made a mistake? Yes, she fell into temptation, but haven't we all?

Eve wasn't perfect, but she *loved* God. She loved Him *so much* that she wanted to be just like Him; after all, imitation is the sincerest form of flattery. The enemy knew that, and he preyed on it. He used her deepest desire against her to get what he wanted, and in doing so, it caused her to lose everything: "You are not enough . . . you could be more. You could be like God."

The serpent, Satan, led her to believe that who she was wasn't good enough, wasn't pleasing to God, or that her life wasn't good enough even though she had all she could ever want or need. He twisted the truth just enough to make it sound like he had her best in mind when really he was trying to destroy her. The most astounding part is it was all based on a lie. He was cunning. He didn't come flat out and tell her what he was up to; he just placed a small enough doubt in her mind, subtle enough to be undetected, and it caused her to question God's own words to her.

Have you ever been there? Have you ever let the whispers of the enemy override the truth of God? Have you let doubts creep into your mind that are just subtle enough to make you question what God really said? It's time to ask the question:

Who told you that?

We've all listened to the enemy at some point or another, whether we realize it or not. We've all made mistakes and believed the lie over the truth, because there was *just enough* doubt, *just enough* convincing, *just enough* of a lie to blind us. The enemy knows our weaknesses. He knows our points of pride. He knows our personal struggles as well as the struggles we face as women growing up in a beauty-obsessed culture. He knows we often compare ourselves and never feel like we measure up. After all, he's been studying us for a long time.

Think about what it must have been like to live in the garden. No sin, sitting and resting with every beautiful and powerful animal imaginable without fear, being at peace with yourself and your husband, creation, and God, with everything at your fingertips. Adam and Eve had favour and blessing from God, yet, in a single moment in time, by one decision, it was all taken away because of one lie, one question, one whisper of doubt: *You are not enough.*

This lie is as old as time itself, and it's the lie we continue to believe because it seems just believable enough to make us question and make us doubt—make us wonder if we truly are enough. If Eve had considered the source or realized she was being lied to, I believe she would have made a different choice. But many times, we don't recognize the lies of the enemy because they sound just too much like they could be true—a half-truth, just believable enough to make us doubt—just close enough to sound like our own thoughts. Possibly. Maybe.

Truthfully, we aren't enough—on our own. Without Jesus, we are a mess, we aren't justified, and we are destined for eternal death. But because of Him, we are qualified and adopted into His family. In Him, we have worth and value because He makes us worthy enough to be chosen, sought after, and bought with a great price. Sometimes, that truth doesn't register in our hearts. There's a paradigm shift that has to take place—we need a revelation of this truth.

NOT PERFECT, BUT PERFECTLY LOVED

I, too, believed that lie that I wasn't enough, just being who God made me. I think we all have, at one time or another, in one area or another in our lives. This age-old lie has been believed by nearly every human on earth, and it seems that with each new generation of women, that lie continues to thrive, impacting the younger generations at faster and greater rates because of increased cultural pressures of perfection. We see it in the measures that women (and men) go to, slicing and scarring their bodies in all kinds of different ways to achieve an ideal that doesn't define who they are—despite them believing it does.

This is why we need to talk about this and talk about it now because the only way to expose a lie is to tell the truth. It's time to rise up, a strong generation of women who aren't afraid to throw the lies of the enemy back in his face and speak the truth to our daughters and female friends and remind them that *they are enough* because God says they are and because of Jesus' sacrifice. He thought so much of us that He was betrayed by one that He loved, to be whipped and beaten, marring his body, punctured by large, metal nails, hung on a cross—tortured unto death. Who else would go through that voluntarily? He could have been rescued at any moment from what He endured, yet He chose that bitter and tortured way to die because

He chose you. He needed to go through that—for you. To rescue you. To have a relationship with you. To give you eternal life.

We are not worthy of what He did because we earned it; we are worthy of His sacrifice because *He* wanted to do it for us. We are not enough in and of ourselves, but we are enough because of Jesus and the grace and mercy He pours out on us—sinners who were once lost in sin but are now found and made righteous through His sacrifice.

We are made perfectly and wonderfully, just the way we are, because we were designed on purpose, for a purpose. Yes, we need to grow in righteousness. Yes, we need to grow in the fruits of the Spirit. Yes, we need to grow in intimacy with God, and we should be seeking to grow in all those areas, but God made you exactly the way He wanted you—perfectly His. The things you see as flaws, He sees as His fingerprint. The things you see as imperfections, He sees as His masterpiece.

Far too often, we look at our outer shell and we critique it, thinking it's not good enough or that it doesn't meet the standard. And honestly, it usually doesn't when we hold it up against the beauty standard of the culture. But where in Scripture are we called to make our bodies idols? We aren't—we are actually told the opposite.

Our bodies are temples—shells that house us, made to honour God—but how often are they used as billboards to promote our pride or shackles built from insecurity that make us feel unloved and unworthy? They shouldn't be used as either.

Where do you fit in the scheme of confidence in who God made you? Are you on one end of the spectrum where you are striving to keep up with the beauty standards, using Botox or surgery to try to keep yourself looking young or thin? Or maybe you're on the other end of the spectrum, believing that you're just plain flawed or unattractive, which just amplifies your insecurities. It doesn't matter which end you're on; they're both fraught with lies and filled with untruths from the enemy—they're both unbalanced extremes.

The goal of this book is to bring you back into balance —right in the middle—guiding you back to God's picture of who He created you to be. That doesn't mean you need to feel condemnation if you have striven for beauty on the outside or feel ashamed because of how you've torn yourself down on the inside, but it does mean it's time to look out from behind the curtain and see what you've been hiding from. Your body isn't meant to define you. If it's taking up that much real estate in your mind, it's time to tell that mind of yours what to focus on instead: who God made you and Whose you are.

See, friend, you're not perfect inside or out, but one thing is for sure: you're *loved* perfectly by a God who is always bringing you into deeper holiness with Him as you draw near to Him. It doesn't matter to Him what size your jeans are or how tall you are. Honestly, it really, really doesn't. He isn't at all concerned with what section of the store you shop in, whether it's petite or plus-size or any size in-between. What He looks at is *you*—your heart, your soul, and your amazing ability to bring Him joy just by being you.

But us? Oh, we definitely look at the exterior rather than the interior many times. We worry about what we are presenting to the world on the outside, and in doing so, we miss what God's doing on the inside. Comparison, competition, vying for first place in your looks, trying to chase your youth—these are all external distractions, and they steal joy rather than give you life.

CAN GOD REALLY USE ME?

I know that I spent many years feeling that my failures were too big, that my flaws were deal-breakers, and I questioned how God could possibly use someone who was so imperfect. Surely, my faults were too great. Surely, what I saw on the outside (or hid on the inside) defined who I was. At one point, I asked myself, who was whispering in my ear to make me believe that God made some kind of mistake with me. Who was I to think that I needed to chase perfection when I know that because of sin, I will always be imperfect until I am made new in glory one day? Whose voice was I listening to that made me believe I had to be a certain way to be loved, that I was a failure, that I wasn't enough for my Father?

Who told me that?

We have picked up flaws as humans, each of us, in unique ways, but Jesus came to save the sinner, not the perfect. I began to recognize that these lies I had believed for so many years were not from my Father but from the accuser of the brethren, Satan. I had allowed his whispers of doubt to lead me to question God's choice in choosing me and His ability to love me without condition.

It's ironic that uniqueness and flaws are sometimes celebrated in inanimate objects but never in people. Certain flaws in wood, such as knots or unique grains, can add value to the object. Small imperfections in antique furniture add character and help fetch a higher price. Yet, when it comes to humanity, we live in a culture that doesn't value human flaws. Personality flaws, physical flaws, conversational flaws, relational flaws—they're all regarded as problematic. But what if they're actually the thorns of the flesh that God uses to draw us closer to Him (2 Corinthians 12:7)? What if these "flaws" are there to help us cast our cares on Him and rely on Him to refine us?

Look how far the world of glamour has taken covering up flaws. Camera filters are almost impossible to avoid now. Young girls are growing up in a society where they feel they're only acceptable if they're seen through a filter —either a physical filter or a psychological one. Flaws are being erased from every part of women's bodies as fast as they can find them. No one should dare expose a mole or a grey hair, an age-spot or a roll. They pretend. They stand behind the curtain. They lock themselves in a room of closets, curtains, and doors, hoping they can shut criticism out, but instead, *life* shuts *them* out, destining them into a prison of isolation and seclusion.

Who told you that?

Satan loves to point out what makes you different from the cultural standard, but he doesn't want you to go to God with it; he'd rather make you feel bad about yourself by piling on shame and guilt. He'd rather you try to hide who you are. He'd rather toss you into a pit of condemnation and rejection—or better yet, he'd like you to do it yourself! If he can convince you to reject yourself, he's won the battle in your mind!

That's exactly what we do when we tear ourselves down—when we shame ourselves, our figures, our age, our financial status, our worth. We give him the day off, and instead, we take over the role of digging that pit for ourselves and throwing ourselves into it. It's time to stop tearing ourselves down to others and to ourselves and learn to see ourselves the way God sees us. It's time to learn to see who we are inside and how God made us, and let that shine through. It's time to speak truth over ourselves instead of lies. It's time to step into the truth of who God has made us to be so that no lie from the enemy can cause us to disbelieve who we are and who God created us to be.

The enemy wants you to believe that your flaws (what the culture claims are flaws, but that's not how God sees them) are irreparable and that you should be ashamed and condemned because of them. He tries to convince you that God would love you *more* if you did everything right—but that's a lie. God will never love you any more or any less than He does right now.

The enemy also doesn't want you to know who you *truly* are. He doesn't want you to know your *true* worth and value, which are found in Christ. He wants you to pull yourself away from God and your relational community and pour on guilt and shame that makes you feel unworthy so that you don't run to your Father to be reminded of just how precious you are to Him. The enemy knows that if you run to your Father, He will tell you exactly who you are, who you were created to be, and what you have as an inheritance in Him. No, Satan doesn't want that at all. He wants you to believe God's love is dependent on your perfection. Pfft.

I say, "Pfft," because his lies may come at you, but

they're never true. Anytime I begin to believe that my flaws (again, what the culture would consider flaws) should cause me to feel shame or rejection, I realize I've allowed the enemy's lies to take root, and that's my cue to reject the lies and speak the truth. That, of course, doesn't mean that we don't repent if there's sin in our lives or if we made a mistake, but what it does mean is that, as His children, we can repent and be forgiven. We don't need to wallow in self-pity and doubt about all the things we've done wrong because we've been forgiven and set free through the power of the cross.

NO MORE LIES

I don't know when exactly it happened in my journey, but at some point near the end, I had an epiphanic moment: I finally stopped believing I was broken and that *this body was a result of my brokenness.* Pause, let that sink in for a moment.

I stopped believing that this new body represented weakness, failure, ugliness, incompleteness, sin, getting what I deserved (recompense, consequence), punishment, condemnation, that my body size was a mistake, or that the enemy had won and this body was the result. Those were all things I had believed when I first began my journey. Sad, isn't it? Those were all lies deposited by the father of lies. He took no shame in trying his best to make me believe my worth was gone. But each lie he told, each time he thought he'd won, was a moment he'd actually lost. He didn't know where I'd go with those lies. He didn't know I would bring them to my Father, that I'd weigh and measure each one with Him. He didn't know that my Father would crush each lie, one by one, and speak the truth in the tenderest of ways. Each one was a moment of growing in intimacy with Him. Each one was a moment of showing His love for me. Each one was a moment of complete stripping away of lies—new lies and very, very old lies—and replacing the lies of the darkness with the truth of the light. Each one was brought to Him, laid before the altar, and lovingly nailed to the cross by my Saviour.

God cannot speak truth into the things we keep from Him. He cannot speak truth into the areas we hide, afraid, in our shame. God will always tell us the truth, but as it says all throughout Scripture, we have to ask. We have to bring the struggles and the things we've been told to the Lord, to weigh and measure them *with Him* and say, "Which one, Lord? Which one is true? Which one is a lie? What do *You* say?"

God isn't afraid of our messes. He's not afraid of the lies we've believed. He's not afraid of our questions or the hard emotions we deal with. He doesn't want us to try and solve it on our own or just believe something at face value; He wants us to bring it to Him, so He can separate bone and marrow, to expose the lies, so He can reveal to us the truth.

When Adam and Eve sinned in the Garden of Eden, their eyes were opened to their sin, and they saw that they were naked. They immediately felt shame, and because of their shame, they hid. When we feel shame, we hide from God. We are so disappointed in ourselves that we run *from* Him, rather than run *to* Him. We let our shame become a barrier between us and God. But just as God behaved with Adam and Eve in the garden, He does the same with us. He looks for us; He runs to us because He doesn't want us to stay hidden in our shame. He wants us to bring our pain and our hurts to Him so He can speak truth where the enemy has spoken lies.

In my shame of what I had felt about my body, I wanted to hide it from God because I was so ashamed to be struggling with it. But I looked ahead to where that path ended, and it was nothing that God had planned for me. It was a path riddled with loneliness, bitterness, self-shame, anger, anxiety, and much more pain. I knew that those weren't the plans God had for me. The only way I could see forward was to bring my shame to Him. And a beautiful exchange happened there: I brought Him my shame, and He brought me truth. He showed me where I had heard lies from the enemy, and then He told me that the lies weren't true and instead told me the truth—about who I was, who He made me to be, and how He sees me. And my friend, it changed everything.

He showed me the truth. Nothing in Scripture says that a "culturally beautiful" body is the result of more blessing or favour, goodness or happiness. He showed me that what Scripture *does* say is that He has incredibly *good* plans for me *and* that He works good out of all the messes in my life, which begs the question He posed: *Why would this situation be any different?* Why would I try to make myself and my body be something that God hasn't ordained it to be, this side of heaven? Why would I try to fit the mold that was never designed for me to fill?

I made a decision then and there. God had given me all the facts. He had laid it all out. He had shown me the truth. Now it was my turn to make the decision—and I did.

I decided no more "when I get there" or "if I get there" when it comes to clothes. No more feelings of shame when something doesn't fit like I expected. No more trying to squeeze myself into things that aren't *designed* to fit my body. No more gazing at thin women and wishing I had what they do. No more asking God to make my body look the way I think it should. No more making myself happy in the way *I* think I'll be happy. No more complicating what God's made simple. No more guessing if He got my body wrong. No more believing I did something wrong to have this body. No more thinking I need to look a certain way to be loved or accepted or *beautiful*. No more. That was it! He did the work, He showed me the truth, but He let *me* decide what I was going to do with it.

HOW DO I FIX THE PATTERN?

In order to stop the pattern of guilt and shame and listening to the lies of the enemy, we need to fill ourselves back up with the truth daily! Yes, it's a daily practice. When the enemy comes at you with lies, recognize *who told you that* and who those lies came from, and then get into the Word and be reminded of the truth. Being filled by the Word of God reminds us of who we are, and it reminds us of the truth. I would *love* it if we could read the Word once and be completely impervious to forgetting the truth or making a mistake, but we have human weaknesses that require the loving grace of our Father to help us grow in righteousness. We are vessels for the Holy Spirit, and as vessels, we need to be filled up daily, because, as I said earlier, we leak. Thankfully, though, we can be filled back up by reminding ourselves of who we are from the truth in God's Word and by praying—putting on the battle gear you can read about in Ephesians 5.

Being tested only reminds me of Who I need to go to for the truth—Jesus, the Author and Perfecter of our faith (Hebrews 12:2). Being tempted by the enemy should not bring guilt and shame, but it should be a reminder of who I need to run to, to remind me of who I am.

When you begin to question who you are—your worth or value—or let shame begin to take up residence in your mind, you can be sure it's the condemning spirit of the enemy who is trying to shake you. The biggest thing you need to remember is that *a lie can never be true*. No matter how many times he tries to tell you that you are a failure, that your job defines your worth, that your weight determines your value, or your socio-economic status measures your importance, *it doesn't make it true*.

Go back to reading and meditating on the truth of God's Word because not only is it powerful, but you can speak that truth back to the enemy and tell him exactly who you are. Remind him *Whose* you are. Let the truth of the Word become so repetitive in your heart that it sinks deep into your soul. Let it become so ingrained in you that when you hear the condemning lies of the enemy, you immediately recognize that they are lies because you're so full of the truth. Study the Word in the area of your worth in Christ, and study what God says about you. We will cover those verses later in this book, and I encourage you to meditate on them and memorize them; don't just read them once and forget.

As you go through your day, I encourage you to pay attention to the thoughts that pop into your head. You don't have to believe them just because they popped in. Oftentimes, when we are stressed or weak, tired or worried, it's an easy entry-point for the enemy to pop in a lie. And when you're tired, you're less likely to recognize negative or untrue thoughts. But the more you practice being aware of what you're thinking about, the more the truth will set you free (John 8:32). When you become aware of a thought that seems negative or untrue, here are some questions to ask yourself immediately to measure it against the truth. Use these questions as a guide to help you begin navigating whether it's the truth or a lie:

1. Does it line up with the Word of God (what God says about you)?

2. Is it condemning (shame, fear, worry) or convicting (correction)? (This takes some discernment, which we will explore later.)

If the answers to these questions are:

1. "No, it doesn't line up with the truth of who God says I am."
2. "Yes, it's condemning and creates shame, fear, or worry."

. . . then it's not from God, and it's a lie. Time to take that thought captive, give it to God, and pray. It's also a good time to get into the Word and be reminded of the truth.

To remember these steps, use the three Rs: *Recognize, Reject,* and *Realign.*

Recognize: Recognize your thoughts and what you're thinking about. Did your mood suddenly change in a negative way? Time to recognize the thoughts that got you there.

Reject: If those thoughts are negative and resonate with the questions above (if they don't line up with God's Word and they lead to condemnation), it's time to reject them as lies.

Realign: Now that you have recognized and rejected the lie, you can't stop there; you have to fill yourself back up with the truth. That means you go to the Word and see what the Word says about it. For example, if the lie is that you feel stupid, you would make a list of verses that speak to that, such as Psalm 139, that you can refer to. Bring all of this to the Lord in prayer.

Typically, there will be areas you know you struggle in, so it's good to have some verses already handy on your phone or journal that you can go to or have them bookmarked in your Bible or highlighted and saved in your Bible app, related to these topics, such as body image, your mind, etc. Throughout the book, there are many great verses you can reference as a guide in relation to these areas, but I also encourage you to look up verses on your own in the areas you struggle with because God's Word is like medicine.

When you recognize negative thoughts, you're stopping whatever wrong thought is being played in your mind, and you're giving it to God so it can't take root. This is exactly what the Bible calls "casting down imaginations." What I'm sharing with you isn't new; it was God's idea first, but the above steps are a broken-down version to help give you practical steps as a guide. It's all based on what Paul said in 2 Corinthians 10:5, that we should be *"casting down imaginations, and every high thing that is exalted against the knowledge of God, and bringing every thought into captivity to the obedience of Christ"* (ASV).

Let *God* tell you what the truth is. Let Him remind you of His promises and the truth about who you are through His Word.

FEELINGS AREN'T OUR GUIDE

We can easily live so much of our lives led by our feelings because feelings are a part of who we are as humans. But when our lives are led by our feelings or emotions, causing us to make decisions based on them, we become passengers on an emotional rollercoaster. Feelings are meant to bring our attention to how we are responding to something and should be an indication to pray, but they're not meant to be a GPS that tells us to react to them or to make knee-jerk-reaction decisions by them. Emotions are a wonderful check engine light, but are a terrible GPS.[8] Stable people are not led by their feelings but are led by fact and truth. Feelings can change so quickly: One moment, you can feel one way, and then seconds later, you can feel a completely different way based on your circumstances or even your mood.

Paul was a wise man of God who understood that we shouldn't let our emotions be led by our circumstances. He tells us in Philippians 4:11–13:

I am not saying this because I am in need, for I have learned to be content whatever the circumstances. I know what it is to be in need, and I know what it is to have plenty. I have learned the secret of being content in any and every situation, whether well fed or hungry, whether living in plenty or in want. I can do all this through him who gives me strength. (NIV)

He *learned* that if he was going to base his peace, joy, or any other emotion on his circumstances, he could not accomplish all that God had for him. I have seen this principle to be so true in my own life!

Our circumstances *will* affect our emotions to a degree —that's a fact—but what we do with those emotions is our choice. We can choose to give in to the emotions and make our decisions based on how we feel, or we can choose to be sober-minded, as Paul says, and not let our emotions rule us. We can pray and cast our worries and cares to God and let Him handle them. Worry is always a signal to pray!

I am not trying to convince you that it will be easy to change how you've done things; it likely won't. It's going to take practice; it will take determination and perseverance, committing to the decision you made and not wavering. But when we learn to put our circumstances in God's hands and fully surrender to Him, it's amazing how the emotions lose their power and become secondary. We have to practice not living by our emotions because they easily fluctuate, and fluctuation makes it difficult to be stable and consistent.

When I was first struggling with my new body size, the enemy used every opportunity to try and cause me to look at what I *wasn't*.

"You *aren't* a certain size."

"You don't look like you used to."

"Clothes shopping is too hard, so why bother?"

"You won't find anything you'll look good in."

"You will never look as good as you used to."

God speaks life, but the enemy speaks lies. These were all lies I heard, and they led to the enemy stealing my joy when I didn't reject them. My mood would change on a dime when I began comparing myself with what I wasn't. It seemed everywhere I turned, I was facing condemnation and shame. It was exhausting. But as I learned to recognize those thoughts as being lies when they popped in, I began to take the ground back from the enemy by *Recognizing, Rejecting,* and *Realigning* them with what God says!

I've heard it said that emotional exhaustion is more tiring than working a full day of physical labour, and seriously, I see why! Listening to the enemy's lies and focusing on what I wasn't was exhausting, and it caused me to be angry and bitter. I gave the enemy a foothold in my mind when I allowed his words to take root rather than rejecting them right away. Remember, Satan's lies can be *just* convincing enough that we believe them, even if only a little—but they'll *never* be true.

I didn't realize I was listening to lies because they sure *felt* true to me. Thoughts turn into emotions, and emotions turn into feelings, but those feelings aren't always accurate, especially if that first thought is based on a lie. Feelings are real and can feel true, but they can also mislead us. Remember, they're a good "check engine light" but not a good GPS to make decisions by. When you start studying the truth about what God says about you and discovering who you *truly* are in Him, it won't take long before you start to recognize the lies of the enemy and notice when he whispers negative thoughts about your appearance or who you aren't. You will learn to reject the lies and fill your mind with the truth.

One example of how emotions and feelings can be misleading was when we got a puppy. I was so excited to finally get the puppy we had been waiting for for over a year. We had been missing our first dog, and it was all I could think about to get another one. Our first dog was the exception to the rule. She was extremely calm and well-behaved. The more I looked at pictures of her and cute puppies on the internet, the more I let my emotions begin to take over. I wasn't giving much thought to how busy we were and the commitments we had made, but instead, I was feeding my emotions by focusing on what I wanted: a dog.

Looking at photos of sweet little puppies for a few weeks was—in retrospect—not a great idea when needing to make a rational (rather than an emotional) decision.

In the weeks leading up to her arrival, I could barely

handle the excitement; the anticipation was great! I wanted her to be home with us so desperately that I could hardly stand it. The night before we had planned to pick her up, I had a hard time sleeping because my excitement had completely taken over.

You may be thinking that excitement isn't a bad emotion, and you're right; it's not. Being misled by your emotions doesn't apply just to the negative ones; it can also be the positive ones that mislead us, sometimes even more so. Even when the emotions are positive ones, we still need to learn to practice not letting them steer us.

The day finally came when our new puppy arrived. The excitement in the home was palpable, and I was so content, knowing the puppy we had waited so long for was finally here.

The first night, she had a hard time settling down to sleep, but it didn't bother me because my "excitement emotions" were still elevated. By the second night of disturbances, I was a little more irritated but still okay with the minor interruptions. By the end of the first week, though, I was losing my patience. Why couldn't she just go to sleep and stop interrupting my sleep?

Then came the non-stop nipping, which was followed by the chewing of everything in her sight. Next, the pull-off-and-rip-the-toilet-paper-roll phase kicked in. My patience wore a little thinner. All of our hands and ankles looked like we had lost a fight with a barbed-wire fence due to all the nips and cuts of her tiny, sharp puppy teeth. She was beyond the typical chewer; she had a slightly aggressive side starting to show.

Suffice it to say, by the end of the second month with her, I was ready to give her back. I was so exhausted, and my patience had run so thin it was invisible. The determination to push through had left me completely. The initial feelings of excitement were long gone, and they were not sustaining me through all the other frustrations. My emotions had drastically changed in a short amount of time, and I found myself in a puddle of tears (on more than one occasion), wondering what on earth I was thinking in getting this mini-terror. I had been led by my emotions in deciding to get a dog, yet those initial emotions were not sustaining me through the difficult circumstances I was encountering.

During that time, I knew I would be working on a massive renovation, and my kids were being homeschooled due to COVID-19, amongst some other busyness that was taking place at the same time. Had I instead thought more rationally about getting a puppy and weighed all the circumstances we had going on in our lives, I would have been able to see with a clear mind that it was not good timing.

Needless to say, for many months, I regretted my decision. I questioned, almost daily, my decision to get her. It led to many tears, a number of demolished items, a lack of patience with my family, more tears, and many frustrated moments that could have been avoided had I not let myself be ruled by my emotions.

And so, as with most things, I learned my lesson from going through it rather than just reading about it. That always seems to be how we do our best learning: by going through something hard and learning from our mistakes. It was a clear reminder to me that I needed to be more cautious about getting caught up in emotions. Emotions have no follow-through. *Positive emotions will not fix bad decisions.* They will not sustain us in the consequences of wrong choices. Eventually, the emotions will shift, and you will be left with a mess to clean up (sometimes quite literally—cue the puppy puddles).

I share that story with you to demonstrate the importance of not being led by emotions and to remind you to question the thoughts that pop into your mind that *are* led by emotions.

Emotions are like wild animals. They're beautiful, and they can add richness to life, but if left untamed and wild, they can be dangerous. When you begin to feel led by your emotions, remind yourself to press pause and think things through rationally. Pay attention to your thoughts. Untamed emotions can cause you to feel things or make decisions that you wouldn't if you weren't clouded by them. Instead, think rationally through things and pray, pray, pray. Ask God to give you discernment and show you the truth, because He will.

Emotions are part of who we are, but when you have a negative script playing in your head about how your body looks, it results in some challenging feelings. It can be incredibly hard in this world of mirrors and filters to feel confident in your skin when the culture around you tells you that you need to look a certain way to be acceptable, but God wants you to love who He created you to be. For some of you, friends, it's going to take some time and some re-programming. The culture and enemy have already had plenty of time to program you to believe you're not enough, that you don't fit the mold, and that you can never be happy again being the size you are, but that's not true. In the following chapters, we are going to explore what God says about you and how you can take back the truth and walk in freedom by understanding who you are, your worth, and your value.

YOU'RE GOD'S HANDIWORK

We all come in many varied shapes and sizes, and I believe God loves to see His creative and diverse design in all of us! Look at nature and the vast diversity of the plants, animals, and stars—the entire universe is a mixture of amazingly different and unique creations.

Then, look at the diversity He designed in us! Look at the multiple colours and shades of skin. No two people are the same. Look at the vast palette of eye colours He crafted, the multiple styles of coils in a hair follicle, or the tanned, freckled skin of some versus the smooth, porcelain skin of others. Notice the array of heights—tall, short, and every height in-between. He designed the plump and the curvy, the fit and the thin. I could go on and on with the variety in which He created all His children. One is not better than another. One style of body or skin colour or skin texture is not superior to Him, despite what the culture will try to have you believe. God doesn't have a favourite body type. He doesn't prefer thin and tanned to plump and porcelain. God doesn't have a style, a preference, or a standard. I know that's hard to believe. We think that the ideal body is the one that the culture says it should be, but God doesn't have a preference! Does that change how you see your body? He thinks we are each special and unique the way He made us—and He's in love with you.

You're unique and uniquely loved because of who He created you to be. There's only one you, and you were *just the one* He had in mind when He created and designed you. God loves to show His diversity in His creation, so it's time we begin to embrace it, too. Flip the script from believing what the culture says about you and what the enemy tries to tell you to what God says about you.

Who told you that?

Listen to what God says, not the enemy. Arm yourself with the truth by studying God's Word to see what He says about you, and spend time praying about it and talking about it with Him. As with anything in life, things don't just get fixed by accident or happenstance; they take work. That means you need to get out some paper, highlighters, and your Bible (or your Bible app) and start studying the Word in the area of your identity in Christ.

We are going to study more about your identity in Christ in chapter 6. Be prepared to take notes! Personally, before I had memorized verses on my identity in Christ, I would put them on my mirror for when I got ready. I would put them around my room and on my phone in my Notes so that I had easy access to them anytime I needed to be reminded of the truth. And when you feel tempted to listen to the enemy's pattern of lies or thoughts, you can *Recognize* them, *Reject* them, and then *Realign* them with who you are in Christ (what God says about you) and, by faith, be filled with truth.

The world has many Band-Aid solutions, but none of them work long-term because they're only temporary fixes. The only way to change how you see yourself is to learn and know how God sees you. Let's begin taking those steps now!

CHAPTER FIVE

Trauma and Identity

W hy is it that we are so easily able to believe the lies but struggle so hard to believe the truth about who we are? Oftentimes, who we are—our identity— is something we take on from external factors, something we adopt because of trauma, or something that someone else says we should be. We pick up these identities along the way, accepting them at face value and allowing them to become part of who we believe we are without questioning them at all. We allow these labels to define us, but we rarely—if ever—stop to ask ourselves what God says.

Trauma is a key piece that can affect what we believe about our identity. All it takes is one lie, one misspoken word, one traumatic event, one idea to take root— especially when we are young—and we are vulnerable to believe it.

"Furry face!" was suddenly hurled in my direction one cloudy day in my fourth-grade classroom. I was quite a shy child—I kept to myself. As is typical of many eight-year-old children, I didn't associate much with the boys. As far as I was concerned, they were from a different planet, and I'd much rather hang out with my female friends.

The taunting started out of the blue. "Furry face! Furry face! Chelsey has a furry face!" I remember feeling my face get really hot, and I'm sure I lit up bright red like a Christmas light. First of all, I thought, why were the boys even talking to me? Boys and girls rarely interacted in our class; like the Montagues and Capulets, there was an unspoken barrier. They didn't talk to us, and we didn't talk to them, yet suddenly, all bets were off. I was so perplexed; why were they being so mean?

I didn't want attention from the boys at all, especially not that kind of attention. Ironically, I didn't have any facial hair whatsoever, so the boys teasing me about having a furry face came completely out of left field. I wanted to ignore their snide remarks, their lewd taunts, and let them roll off my back, but I was a kid—a young girl—naive and unaware, suddenly realizing my appearance was something to be aware of, something I could be made fun of for. It was the first time I had ever thought about my looks. Before that, I just did what I did because I liked it, with no thought of anyone ever calling me out or rejecting me because of it. It was the first time I felt insecure about my looks—the first time I had even paid attention to them.

The boys' taunting really affected me and made me feel odd, unusual, and rejected. For the first time, an insecurity about my looks began to form under the surface. As with most insecurities that burrow into our lives, it was based on a lie, yet it became my truth simply because I believed it.

I jumped into the car after school, crying and pouring my tears out to my mom on the ride home in our grey Honda Civic, looking for consolation. "They're just teasing you because they like you," she said. And although I understood that she was consoling me the best way she knew how, it didn't remove the stinger that had lodged its way into my heart. The venom had already begun to seep into my being, piercing through the skin, circulating its way through my blood, and pulsing through my veins, shifting the fabric of who I was. The nickname continued for what seemed like months. I don't remember when the nickname stopped, but what I do remember is that it was the first time I began to feel self-conscious about my looks. It was the first time I realized I could be judged on my looks—what a stark and sad realization for an eight-year-old little girl.

Throughout the years, that wound stuck around. I

didn't think about it all the time, but the lie that I had believed—that began with the taunting—was that I was different, odd, and an outcast. I began to believe that my outer appearance was the only thing people saw, and it mattered more than my inner self. The lie I believed was that I was rejected—rejected because of my looks, something I didn't know was possible at eight years old. Those lies began to layer more and more as I grew up.

Craig Groeshel, author of *Winning the War in your Mind* and pastor of Life Church in Oklahoma, says, "*Your life is always moving in the direction of your strongest thoughts.*"[9] And he's right. The more you dwell on those thoughts, the more they grow into other similar thoughts and branch out from there. And before you know it, you've got an entire root system of beliefs, built on a lie, and these lies spread out into new areas of your life.

The experiences and the beliefs we have are an accumulation of thoughts and events, so if we begin with a lie, that lie continues to grow new lies, and eventually, we believe that lie must be true. I believe this is one of the foundational cycles that begins the process of insecurity—believing a lie and adding more lies to that without realizing it because it's a process that happens in our thoughts, and often, we aren't aware of our destructive thought patterns.

Young, eight-year-old me struggled to comprehend what was happening, and in doing so, I had begun to believe the lie that I should be concerned about my appearance and that I could be rejected for it. That lie played out in my life over the proceeding years. I didn't recognize it was a lie that needed to be uprooted, but instead, I let it inadvertently grow new branches, leaves, and roots of similar lies. That wasn't, of course, the only thing that contributed to my insecurity about my looks, but it was a pivotal point as to where it began.

At one point or another, we have all faced insecurity—whether it's a job we don't feel qualified for, comparing ourselves with someone else, or questioning the decisions we make. Insecurity can be circumstantial, but it's often a result of a deep-seated belief (based on a lie) that we have believed about ourselves.

The enemy is "*the accuser of our brethren*" (Revelation 12:10 KJV). That's us—the brethren. His goal is to attack and accuse us and to point out and prey upon our weaknesses. He doesn't want us to grow in faith; he wants to squash it. He doesn't want us to trust in God; he wants to convince us we are on our own and need to figure things out in our own strength. That is one of the biggest lies that we need to expose and stand against, because once we realize it is a lie, it loses its power.

Once you recognize that you're struggling with insecurity in some area, you need to begin looking at the root causes of your insecurity. Insecurity is *always* a result of a lie that you have believed. It's either through trauma that has happened to you (which you have taken on as your identity), through the condemning words of someone that the enemy has used, or believing lies that the enemy whispers to you. Once you believe those lies to be true (without recognizing they are lies), it's easy for the enemy to begin turning those lies into giants in your life. A giant lie can have devastating effects on one's mental and even physical health.

FACING YOUR GIANTS

When we think of King David in the Bible, we often think of a man after God's own heart. We picture a strong king who wrote many of the Psalms and lived a great life (minus his famous indiscretion with Bathsheba), but David didn't necessarily have an easy life. God needed to prepare him for the throne, and in doing so, David had to face some giants. I mean, it's a little funny—could God have picked a shorter person to fight the giant Goliath? Is it perhaps exactly why God chose to make David small in stature, to drive home the point that it's not by our might or power but by God's Spirit (Zechariah 4:6) and that He can use anyone to accomplish His works? Not only did David have to face Goliath, but he also spent a large portion of his life running from King Saul, who was trying to kill him. He needed to rely on God to be his rock and his rescue through it all, but I believe that's exactly what made David a man after God's own heart. Like David, we don't grow in the easy times; we grow in the hard ones.

We don't read a lot about how David *felt* about facing Goliath, but I have to imagine it was very intimidating. And facing your insecurities (which can feel like giants) can be very intimidating.

Learning to deal with the root causes of insecurity is much like a snake that sheds its skin. In fact, the parallel is so similar that it's quite astonishing. Let's compare.

Snakes shed their skin because they can't continue to grow larger if they stay in their old skin. Part of the reason that snakes shed is because they're growing. Their skin isn't elastic enough to grow with them, so they need to shed the smaller skin as they begin to outgrow it.

When Christ comes to live in our hearts and minds, He becomes a part of us. His nature lives inside of us, and He constantly renews us. The Bible says, "*Though outwardly we are wasting away, yet inwardly we are being renewed day by day*" (2 Corinthians 4:16 NIV). God is showing us a better way to live for our benefit because He wants us to grow in Him. However, if we ignore what the Holy Spirit is saying and continue in our old ways, we can't grow, just like the snake can't grow while in its old skin. Insecurity is much like the old skin—it keeps us trapped. It keeps us immature. But as we partner with God to uncover our insecurities and work through them, He creates a new nature and a "new skin" underneath. He is teaching new concepts and showing us the truth about who we are—thus helping us grow into the image of Christ and allowing us to outgrow our old, immature ways of thinking.

Snakes shed their skin to remove parasites that have attached to their skin over time. Parasites attach themselves to a host and feed off of the host. They have no benefit to the host, they *rob* the host of nutrients, and they cause disease that deteriorates the host's health over time.

Lies are the same. Lies are from Satan, and they always seek to tear us down. They rob us of so many things: joy, peace, worth, knowing who we are in Christ—the list goes on. Lies attack our minds and hearts and can lead to sadness, worry, self-doubt, and a lack of worth, but they can even lead us to such emotional distress that they can negatively affect our physical bodies.

Parasites and lies are really one and the same. They both rob, and they both destroy. In order for snakes to get rid of the parasites, they have to shed their skin. They cannot simply shake or knock the parasites off; they have to remove their entire outer skin in order to get rid of the parasite.

Similarly, we have to know the truth in order to get rid of the lies. Just like the snake is preparing new skin underneath, God is revealing new life—the truth—to us. Once the truth has taken root, we can reject the lies, just like the skin of the snake that is removed along with the parasites. The snake prepares the new layer of skin underneath before shedding the old one. Likewise, God waits until we are ready to hear the truth before we can understand our former beliefs about ourselves are actually lies. He waits for the right time. He doesn't push us before we are ready, and His timing is always perfect—you can trust that.

In order to remove the old skin, the snake must rub against something hard to dislodge it. What an incredibly insightful parallel, but it's one that we would rather not face, I'm sure. The snake cannot just slip the old skin off like a pair of socks; it has to work incredibly hard over a period of time to writhe free of the old skin. The snake creates a tear near its head to start the process of removing the old skin and then rubs against a rock—or something hard—until the old skin is fully removed.

Sometimes, we have to go through hard things in order to see the truth. For example, if you've been a victim of abuse, it's not easy to begin counselling or deal with the trauma of the past. It seems daunting and scary to begin unearthing past hurts, but it's the only way to truly heal. Much like the snake must rub against something hard to reveal the new skin, we have to deal with the hard parts of our past in order to walk through the stages of healing, toward freedom. It's not easy for us (or the snake), but in order to grow and be free from the old skin—the old lies, the old insecurities—it's a necessary process.

God is always in the restoration business, and He wants to dispel the lies (shed the skin) so you can grow into the truth of who He says you are. This is so that you can be confident and secure and radiate the joy of the Lord in your life.

You *can* hide behind your curtains and doors or your old skin if you really want to, but eventually, you will grow weary of the obscurity and darkness. Our desire is to be fully known and know that we are fully loved just as we are—both by people and by God. No one can live a lie and be happy, full of joy, or at peace with themselves or God.

THE TRUTH ALWAYS COMES OUT

A Donkey found a Lion's skin left in the forest by a hunter. He dressed himself in it, and amused himself by hiding in a thicket and rushing out suddenly at the animals who passed that way. All took to their heels the moment they saw him.

The Donkey was so pleased to see the animals running away from him, just as if he were King Lion himself, that he could not keep from expressing his delight by a loud, harsh donkey squeal. A Fox, who ran with the rest, stopped short as soon as he heard the donkey's voice. Approaching the Donkey, he said with a laugh:

"If you had kept your mouth shut you might have frightened me, too. But you gave yourself away with that silly squeal."[10]

What is inside always comes out. We can try to hide behind designer labels, expensive cars, perfect bodies, or a 5-star social media persona, but eventually, who you are— what is inside—will reveal itself. I don't say this to worry or threaten you but to make you stop and think. Are you hiding behind things because you don't like who you are inside or because you're trying to hide yourself out of fear of being fully known? You could probably continue this way on the surface for some time, but eventually, one of two things will happen: the real you will come out, or you will become so dissatisfied with being fake that you will sink deeper into unhappiness.

I shared the story earlier of the beautiful tidal wave of healing that God gave to me through a powerfully prophetic dream. It was because of the journey He took me on that I was able to experience such freedom. But the past hurts that led me to that place were hard to face.

Being called furry face in the fourth grade wasn't the worst thing that happened to me. Many hard things had taken place in my life that left me feeling damaged. The abuse I went through as a young child, being friends with someone who didn't treat me well and used mind games to torment me—among other things. Each one left a wound that went undetected for a long time, but the wounds didn't heal over time; they just stayed there, festering below the surface, not brazen enough to be detected.

As a result of that, I learned not to trust people close to me, and that hurt many of my future relationships. I learned to hide behind the curtain of obscurity because I was afraid if anyone found out what had happened to me, they'd think I was damaged, so I did my best to blend in and hide, but at the same time, I wanted so badly to fit in because I felt so unworthy. I was trying to fill God-shaped holes with world-shaped solutions.

I know so many women have faced trauma in their past, some much harsher and longer than I did. Maybe you're one of those women who has faced unimaginable trauma, and mine pales in comparison. But God doesn't only fix the really hard stuff or the really easy stuff; He fixes it all. He asks us to bring it *all* to Him and leave it at the altar. But no matter how long or short the trauma lasts, no matter how little or how much it happened, no matter how extreme or minimal it was, *it all leaves a wound.*

Why a wound and not a scar? A scar indicates healing, but trauma that isn't dealt with doesn't heal *until* it's dealt with; it just stays an open, festering wound. That's often the place where we learn to suppress our feelings and hide who we are because the accuser (Satan) comes in with shame. He pours so much shame on God's daughters in an attempt to make them believe they have no worth or value and by making them believe they're damaged, that they should be ashamed of who they are, that no one would ever want them—at least, not if anyone knew the truth about who they really were. Lie after lie gets piled on, and before long, the wound is festering and gaping. They try to cover it up so no one will see, but all the while, they are living with an open wound that won't heal.

My wound was my sense of worth. It was a wound that was dug with the shovel of deceit, and it needed a God-sized backhoe to fill it in. There was nothing the world or success or anyone could offer me that would properly fill that hole, despite trying everything I could to make myself feel worthy of God's goodness.

As a teen, I thought that if I could just be seen as valuable to male peers, that would fill it. So I sought my worth by trying to get attention from them, but the hole was still there.

Then, as a young adult, I thought if I could just make myself look pretty enough to fit in with the "cool kids," I would feel worthy and accepted. So I strived to fit in by making myself acceptable on the outside, but the hole was still there.

As I went into my late twenties, I thought if I could just be the "perfect" wife, mother, or teacher, maybe then I'd feel like I'd done enough to be valuable, but the hole was still there.

I thought maybe if I did everything right and made everyone around me happy (people pleasing), then I'd feel worthy and accepted, but the hole was still there.

I was desperate to fill the hole, so I continued my quest for worth by thinking that if I was a good enough Christian, maybe God would see that I was worthy of Him, and He'd be proud of me, worthy of meeting the bare minimum standards to let me in. I strived to do everything right and to not make mistakes, but the hole was still there.

Mask after mask, curtain after curtain, I had tried them all. I had tried to be everything to everyone, yet I was missing out on being *myself*—the person God created thirty-nine years ago. I kept trying to put a pretty Band-Aid over the gaping wound, hoping it would hide the truth. I was a wounded patient in need of a doctor, a scared little girl who needed to know her heavenly Father loved her and would protect her.

I strived wholeheartedly for acceptance, not wanting anyone to know anything about my past, my mistakes, or my sins, because I already felt so unworthy. I continually heard the words "damaged goods" play through my mind for most of my life until God brought me into His throne room of redemption through this journey. In that room, He stripped away *all* the things that I had tried to cloak myself with. All the masks came off, the curtains I hid behind were ripped down, and I came before the Lord, naked and poor. No pretense, no veil—just, exposed. I knew that if I was going to ever find true freedom—the freedom in Christ I believed in but hadn't yet experienced—I couldn't hide anymore. I couldn't cower behind masks and curtains, doors and facades—I had to let Him gently take them all away, no matter how scary that seemed.

It was a scary prospect before I began because I knew it wouldn't be easy. I knew it would mean saying goodbye to the safety blanket I had hidden myself behind. I knew it meant being authentic with my Maker and myself, and I knew it meant I couldn't run from the past pain anymore; I had to face it. But the Lord knew my trepidation, and after He stripped all the junk away, the first thing He did when I threw myself at His feet, naked and weak, was cloak me with His love. He got down to my level on the floor of His throne room, bent His knee, leaned toward my downcast face, and with His tender hand, He lifted my chin to gaze into His beautiful face. He told me I am His—that He wants me, that He chose me, and that I belong to Him.

He told me how much He loves me. He told me how I am safe and protected by Him. He told me all the things I needed to hear but was too afraid to let in before. And then He just held me for a long time. He wrapped me in His strong arms and let me rest while He started the process of walking me through my past hurts and into the freedom of healing and peace that only He brings. My freedom journey wasn't overnight, and it felt long at times, but it was always tender and always exactly what I didn't know I needed.

So there I lay, naked and stripped of all the masks I had tried to wear, when my Saviour stooped down from His heavenly throne to see me. *Me.* The real me, not the mask, the actress, or the facade I'd tried to make. Just me. He didn't stoop down to help me because of anything I'd done. He didn't do it because He *had* to. He didn't do it because it's His job or obligation or because He figured He should. It wasn't because it was His duty as my Creator or for any reason other than He loves me and He wanted better for me—He wanted to redeem and restore me.

I was on the run for so many years that when I finally surrendered the baggage of my past to Jesus, I was ready for whatever that looked like. I knew my rescue might not look like I expected, but I knew it was what I *needed*. And it didn't look the way I expected. I didn't expect all the curtains and masks to be stripped away, but even while that process was taking place, I knew it was what I needed. I knew it was good, even though it was really hard at times.

I realized I could live my life wounded, or I could allow Him to step in and heal me. The choice was mine. He wasn't going to *make* me do anything, but a loving Father will always pursue His child in hopes that she will believe He knows what's good for her.

God started my healing journey with the most important cloak (love), but as time went on, He dressed me in many other beautiful robes that restored me. He dressed me in redemption. He dressed me in my true identity in Him, showing me who I truly was as His child, created in His image. He taught me about His character and His goodness *in all things,* even when it sometimes confused my finite mind. He replaced my ragged, filthy rags of self-striving and mistaken identities with glorious robes of royalty that reflected the true identity of my Creator, my Father, my Friend.

He began to slowly fill in all the holes that I had dug, and friend, He was so gentle. He didn't judge me for the amount of holes I had. He didn't look at all the holes I'd dug for myself and make me feel shame for digging them. He simply began to just fill them, hole by hole. Each time He poured a scoop into the hole, it was a new level of truth in Him and freedom from the lies of the enemy.

When we try to fill our holes ourselves, we often use weak substitutes—grass and straw. These could be food, wealth, beauty, or social ladder climbing, but they don't last. God, however, fills them with something that cannot be destroyed, something that will last forever—our identity and His character. Where are those holes now? They're cemented in, friend! *He filled the holes of my insecurity with the truth of my identity,* which moth or rust cannot destroy.

When He had finished filling all the holes, He lovingly patted the last shovel-full of cement down and said, "It's finished." No judgment, no debt, just love.

Hopefully, I have learned my lesson, and I won't foolishly dig more holes in the future, but even if I do, I know He will lovingly walk me through filling those as well. You are not a mistake or accident; you are not a nuisance to God. He loves to come in and restore what has been stolen from you and give you freedom from your past and hope for your future. It's not just what He does; it's His joy to do it for you because He delights in you. Learning to let go of the pressure to fit in on the outside releases you to begin leading from the inside.

CHAPTER SIX

Finally Seeing Your Worth

*PS: It Was There All Along

Alarms. Social media posts. Reels. Emails. Phone notifications. Doorbells. Meetings. TV shows. Events. In such a fast-paced world, it's not hard to see why we struggle with quiet, rest, and having time to sort through our thoughts. Our minds run at lightning speed, and being incredibly busy and on the go means we neglect to take the time to assess our thoughts.

It's no wonder then why we struggle to hear God's voice, to hear what He says about us—to silence the noise around us long enough to listen to His whisper of confidence, His whisper of peace, or His whisper just letting you know how much He loves you.

Sometimes, it seems that the enemy shouts the lies in our ears while the Holy Spirit requires pause, rest, and closeness. When we are consumed with busyness and not prioritizing time in the Word or time in prayer, the lies can easily go undetected and can begin to take root.

Believe me, I get it. It can be incredibly challenging to find the time. We definitely have seasons of busyness that demand more of us, but even in those seasons of busyness, somehow, we always find—or rather, make—the time for the things that are most important to us.

Spending time with God is not only important for your walk with Him, but it's vital to learn about Him, His character, and who He is. It's vital to your relationship with Him. It's vital to change the script of negativity that's been running in your head. It's vital to help you see the difference between what culture is telling you versus what God is. It's vital to change how you see yourself. It's vital to learn how He sees you. It's vital to *you*.

I'm sure you've heard a million times the importance of spending time with God, but maybe you haven't understood the reasons behind it. If you don't understand why it's so important to spend time with God, you're unlikely to make it a habit or change anything in your priority list or schedule to make it happen.

The *why* behind the importance of spending time with God is simple: You will get to know Him—your Creator—intimately. When you want to get to know someone better, you spend time with them. It's a spiritual discipline—one that's very important.

Say you meet someone new at an event. Perhaps you have some mutual friends, and you've heard about this person before, but it's your first time meeting them in person. You realize you will likely run into this person again, and you've heard such great things about them that you decide you want to get to know them better. You start by spending a little bit of time with them at the party. You ask them questions about their life. You share parts of your life. You ask about their job or what kinds of things they like. Perhaps you find common ground on a subject and that gets you even more invested in who they are as a person. The more time you spend with them, the more you get to know about them and the more you realize if you want to get to know them more or not.

In other circumstances with, say, a friend, if time or space prevents you from seeing that friend, it's not as if you *stop* being friends, but it is harder to maintain depth in the friendship. When you *do* get a chance to see them again, it's often as if no time has passed, and you can pick back up where you left off. However, you might miss out on knowing what kinds of things are going on in their life because you haven't stayed in touch.

If too much time passes without staying in touch, you begin to drift apart. It's not that you want to drift apart, but without the investment of time spent with them, they become less of a priority in your life. If weeks turn into months and months into years, you may find you struggle to know them as well as you used to. This is true in any relationship, even one as close as a marriage. An investment of time with people is what creates depth in relationships.

The same is true of our time with God. The more time we spend with Him, the more we learn about Him: His character, who He is, and how He operates. We also get to know more about ourselves: who we are, our purpose, and *identity*.

God is our Creator, our Sculptor, our Inventor, our Artist. He knew exactly what and who He was making when He made you, so it stands to reason that the One who designed and created you is the One who knows you best: perfectly and intimately.

The culture around us has assaulted so many things about our identity, but we cannot look to the culture around us to be our barometer on what is good or right, true or false. We cannot look to the culture to tell us who we are—that's God's job.

COMPARISON

To say that comparison is a thief is a gross understatement. Comparing ourselves with others—either feeling less than someone else or better than someone else—robs the very depths of who we were created to be because it causes us to either believe we are less than we should be or that we are better than we are. It steals our identity. We don't need to look and act like someone else; we were made uniquely!

The message that we need to conform to what the culture says we should be is a farce. In fact, it is in direct opposition to what the Word of God teaches. Romans 12:2 says that we need to have our minds *transformed and renewed* by Christ rather than *conformed* to the culture around us. We are made in the image of God, and we should strive to be like Him and not like the world. Philippians 2:5 says we should *"have the same mindset as Christ Jesus"* (NIV). Nowhere in the Bible does it say that we should imitate or conform to what the culture around us dictates; as I just showed you, it says the opposite!

We don't need to mimic or envy any human here on earth, but we *are* called to be more like Christ. We are called to a higher standard than merely blending in or conforming our bodies to match the world around us. We *should* stand out. We *should* be set apart. Does that mean you can't style your hair or wear fashionable clothes? Not at all—but I do implore you not to let your body become an idol in your life.

God hasn't called us to live up to the cultural standards; He's called us to be a people after His own heart. When you read what Jesus did while He was on the earth, He didn't spend or waste His time beautifying people on the outside. He spent His time serving His

Father, teaching people about how to be more like God, fixing the problems in their lives, and teaching them service, kindness, and love.

We are all called to do those same things here on earth —to emulate Jesus. That doesn't mean we can't get our hair done or wear nice clothing. We don't have to go all "John the Baptist" on ourselves—eating locusts and living in the desert with loin cloths as our only garments—but we do need to care *more* about the inside than the outside. Just like God does. Just like it says in 1 Samuel 16:7, *"Man looks on the outward appearance, but the LORD looks on the heart."* We need to look at the heart, too. Our own heart. And ask the Holy Spirit to show us who we are, where we need to grow, and how we can show God's heart to the culture around us.

We can't do that if we aren't set apart. Being set apart doesn't mean being plain or never wearing make-up or jewelry, but it does mean that we don't lead with our exterior; we lead with our interior. We lead with the Holy Spirit who lives inside us. We lead with integrity. We lead with the love of God for people. We lead with the things that God says are important instead of the things the culture says are important because those two things will *always* be opposites. Some days, it can be hard. Being set apart is a call to holiness that doesn't often come with an easy road, but it's a good road.

SET APART

When I read about the Israelites in the Old Testament, and all the rituals and rules and laws they had to live by to be considered holy before the Lord, I get exhausted just reading about it. I cannot imagine trying to actually walk it out. They had to live sinless lives, which was impossible, and God knew that. In order to allow them to be made right again with Him, God had to put a sacrificial sacrament in place, which was burning sacrifices on His altar.

The Israelites needed to be a beacon of holiness to those around them—to be set apart from the culture of sin and evil. If they lived lives like everyone else, how would anyone know they were God's people? How would anyone know what was good and holy or evil and sinful if they didn't have the law? How could anyone see a difference in them and want to turn away from their sinful life if they weren't shown it by how the Israelites behaved? They had to stand out, not by how they looked but by how they lived.

Fast forward to today's culture; it is still true that we need to be set apart from the way the culture does things if we want to be a witness to the world around us.

Jesus was the first one to preach that we should love our enemies rather than hate them. No other religion had ever taught that. That is counter-culture, especially nowadays in the political and social climate we live in. All other religions are about self, not selflessness. But friends, even after all this time, Jesus is *still* the *only* one who preaches that we should deny ourselves and love our enemies. Why? Because Jesus' words often taught the opposite actions of the culture around them—selflessness rather than self, godliness rather than selfishness. Loving rather than hating. Helping rather than hurting. Saving the lost rather than saving self.

The same is true for us as Christians today. We cannot live like those around us and expect to be set apart and used in powerful ways by God. We cannot behave like the world and then be surprised when they don't see the light shining in us. Jesus spoke to the culture of the day with love but also with truth. We need to do the same.

Your inner man is what should stand out. Jesus says in Matthew 5:13–15 that we should be salt and light. What does that mean? Salt represents making people thirsty for what we have (Christ), and light represents leading people out of the darkness in which they live toward the light (Christ). If we try to imitate the world around us, we will have a hard time being salt or light because we will be striving after all the same things the world is striving after; *we will not stand out if we are mimicking the culture around us*. When we, instead, walk the path God set before us, stand firm in our faith and what we believe, and are thankful for the body in which God placed us, we are speaking much more boldly to the heart of the women we come in contact with.

What speaks to the heart of a woman is not how many people think she is pretty or thin or that she has all the right clothing or home decor. On the surface, that may seem appealing to some women, but deep down, there's something much more profound she is longing for—there's something missing, unsatisfying, and unfulfilling in achieving all of that.

What speaks to the heart of *every* woman is being seen for who she really is inside, being loved just as she is, being accepted for who she is, and seeing purpose in her life. Every *single* woman on the planet wants—no, *needs* —all those things. I would argue every single human, male or female, needs those things.

There is a beautiful exchange that takes place when you spend time with God: You learn more about who He is, and He teaches you more about who you are—your gifts, your unique abilities, your calling, your purpose—who He created you to be. God breaks through all the lies when you spend time with Him, reading His Word and learning about who *He* says you are, who *He* created you to be, and that He *loves* your uniqueness. What makes *you* beautiful is that you're an original—God's own design.

DESIGNED ON PURPOSE

Have you ever painted a painting, completed a beautiful do-it-yourself project, or put together an eye-catching outfit and have been complimented on it? It feels good, doesn't it? Because it's something you designed and created. You have ownership over it because it's unique and it's yours—it came from your imagination and creativity!

In a much more profound and deeper way, that's how God feels about you. He *loves* those freckles you try to cover up. He perfectly blended the shade of green in your eyes and dusted them with tiny flecks of gold. He loves that you belly laugh in the unique way you do when something is funny—He's delighted by it. He relishes in seeing you play in the water with your kids—He's not checking your swimsuit size. He knew it was good when He picked that unique shade to colour your hair and textured it with waves and curls that tickle your face when the wind blows. He was excited to design the most inner parts of your personality, creating you with a dash of humour and a sprinkle of adventurousness. He took time when He picked out the kind of personality you would have, your likes and dislikes, your idiosyncrasies, your quirks, the way you like to make your bed, and how you bite your bottom lip when you're intensely reading a book. He loves the way you slurp your soup (even though everyone else around you may not). He is truly delighted at the creation that is *you* and all your intricacies. What *you* look like is *His* work of art—incredibly beautiful. All these things He designed and created because He knew it was good. He knew He would enjoy watching you grow, but more than that, He knew you were exactly what the world needed.

We are so much more than a mere body here on the earth. We are here for a purpose. Hear me, friend. If you're here and you're alive, it's because God put you here for a purpose. God designed each of us with a unique task in front of us. That doesn't mean everyone is designed to be a preacher or stand on a stage and sing—in fact, very few are. That doesn't mean if you're not doing full-time church ministry, you're wasting your time—not in the least. For so many of us, our ministry is everyday life. If we are intentional, we are ministers in our neighbourhoods, the grocery store, and our kids' basketball team. These are some of the ways that we are salt and light to the community around us. If God wanted us all to be preachers on a stage, who would be there to reach the people who have never or will never set foot in a church? Who would be there to talk to the agnostic who doesn't want anything to do with God but *loves* to share about his son as he watches him learn guitar? We underestimate the ways we can impact the world around us as beacons of light, but we won't walk that out if we all look the same, talk the same, and act the same as the world around us. Our job is often covert; it's living and doing life together while also sharing the message of hope to those around us by how we live.

Resting and spending time with God has a profound effect on how we see ourselves and how we relate to the world around us. It reminds us of our identity, who we really are, who we were created to be, and who God says we are rather than the culture.

The voice we listen to the most often is the one that has the most effect on us. It affects how we feel or see ourselves. There are many voices coming at us. The voice of God, the voice of the enemy, the voices of other people, and our own voice. The voice you listen to determines what you will begin to speak or think about yourself, so it's important which voice you listen to: the enemy's or God's.

What you say or believe about yourself has a profound impact on how you respond to God. For example, if you believe you're unworthy of God's love, you will have a hard time (or maybe an impossible time) receiving God's love for you. Or if you're incredibly hard on yourself and don't believe you deserve forgiveness, you will have a hard time (or a nearly impossible time) forgiving others. What you *believe* about yourself and *say* to yourself has a profound impact on how you relate to God and the world around you. If you've allowed the lies of the enemy to infiltrate your beliefs and thoughts, you will further distance yourself from God. That's why it's incredibly important to realize whose voice you're listening to.

The good news, though, is that even if you have listened to the enemy's voice in the past or even if you are listening in the present, you can change that. It's also good news that even if you've believed the lies of the enemy, it doesn't change who you are—you just need to learn the truth about yourself. You can begin now to understand who you are in Christ. It doesn't take a degree or require any money. All that's needed is some time studying the Word and prayer. Pretty amazing, isn't it, that because of the Holy Spirit, everything we need is available to us, free and accessible?

WHO DOES GOD SAY YOU ARE?

We will never be truly content until we stop comparing ourselves. We will never know who we are until we stop wishing to be like someone else, and the only One who can speak to who we truly are is our Father, our Creator, our Author, our Inventor. Yet the question begs to be asked: Why do we so easily let others convince us of our identity? Who does God say we are? Who does God say *you* are?

You may have heard it said before that our identity is in Christ. I had heard that many times in my Christian upbringing, but I struggled to comprehend what it meant. I hadn't really even thought about it; it was just one of those phrases I had filed away in my mind without any context or real understanding of it. It was one of those "Christianese" phrases I'd heard over and over again, but I don't know if I'd ever really been taught about it or studied it before, so the phrase carried no meaning to me.

Who you are is where you find your worth because it is what defines you. Things of value, like rare coins, are only valuable if the bearer or purchaser knows their worth. To a collector who knows its worth, its value could be thousands of dollars, but to an eight-year-old little boy who just likes the design on the front, it's worth little more to him than a simple trinket that brings him joy. The value is in the eye of the beholder.

Our beholder is God. He's the One who created us, and He's the One who gets to define us and our worth—despite so many people seeking their worth in all the wrong places. And because we know that God cannot lie, who He says we are *is* who we are. We can trust and believe that truth, even if it takes time for our feelings to catch up with our faith.

As we explore who God says we are below, you'll find that some of these things you might resonate with immediately, whereas others may take some time for you to fully resonate with. When we are learning something new, it can take time for us to accept that truth because many emotions, feelings, and thoughts may have been established beforehand that make you feel otherwise. Thankfully, feelings aren't always accurate (and can be changed), but the *truth* is solid and consistent—it's always true, 100 percent of the time! Don't let your feelings lead you astray. Make a choice to believe it because it's true—from God's Word—not based on whether you feel like it's true for you or not. We have to first unlearn the lies before we can learn the truth—kind of like reprogramming your mind. There's also a difference between head knowledge and heart revelation. Pray and meditate on these truths and let them move from head to heart.

I can tell you that you *are* all the things He says you are. If God said it, it's true, because His Word is true.

These statements below are compiled from God's Word to help give you a full picture of who you are and *Whose* you are. It's *absolute* truth—not relative. It's not *your* truth (a false idea that the culture continually tries to make people believe—that truth is something that is fluid and different for everyone). It is *the* truth from the infallible Word of God. Take time to read through them slowly and really digest what they're saying. Even if it takes time, and you have to read and reread them multiple times, take the time to accept these truths as yours because they are yours, as a son or daughter in Him. This is your lineage, your inheritance, your identity. This is who God calls all of His children, those who are in Him.

Each of these truths could be their own book in their own right, but for the sake of time, we will touch lightly on each one. I encourage you to study each of these truths in your own personal study and prayer time with God.

You are God's CHILD—first and foremost. You were an orphan, but you've been adopted by your Father.

Since the beginning of time, you were chosen by God to forever be His child, and that will never change. No matter how many mistakes you make, He still chooses you and will until the end of time. He loves you as much today as He did the moment you were born. He will never love you any more or any less than He does right now, and that love will never change. You're His. Plain and simple. Bought and paid for. All in.

But to all who did receive him, who believed in his name, he gave the right to become children of God. (John 1:12)

We love because he first loved us. (1 John 4:19)

But even before I was born, God chose me and called me by his marvelous grace. Then it pleased him to reveal his Son to me so that I would proclaim the Good News about Jesus to the Gentiles. (Galatians 1:15–16 NLT)

In the beginning was the Word, and the Word was with God, and the Word was God. He was with God in the beginning. Through him all things were made; without him nothing was made that has been made. In him was life, and that life was the light of all mankind. (John 1:1–4 NIV)

You are VALUED—you are of utmost importance, and He takes great care in taking care of you.

God takes great care to look after you, to make sure your needs are met, and to walk beside you in whatever you face or are going through. He will never leave you or turn His back on you. He loves to bless you and give you favour in your life.

He takes great care in every detail of your life, down to how many hairs you have on your head (Matthew 10:30). He gives His angels command to watch over you. "*For he will command his angels concerning you to guard you in all your ways. On their hands they will bear you up, lest you strike your foot against a stone*" (Psalm 91:11–12). There is nothing He won't do to take care of His children, and you are always under His watchful eye.

For we are God's masterpiece. He has created us anew in Christ Jesus, so we can do the good things he planned for us long ago. (Ephesians 2:10 NLT)

Fear not, for I am with you; be not dismayed, for I am your God; I will strengthen you, I will help you, I will uphold you with my righteous right hand. (Isaiah 41:10)

For you formed my inward parts; you knitted me together in my mother's womb. I praise you, for I am fearfully and wonderfully made. Wonderful are your works; my soul knows it very well. My frame was not hidden from you, when I was being made in secret, intricately woven in the depths of the earth. Your eyes saw my unformed substance; in your book were written, every one of them, the days that were formed for me, when as yet there was none of them. (Psalm 139:13–16)

Cast your burden on the LORD, and he will sustain you; he will never permit the righteous to be moved. (Psalm 55:22)

See also Genesis 1:26–27; 5:1; 9:6; and James 3:9.

You are made in GOD'S IMAGE—with all the attributes of a righteous heart.

You are not made in the same physical form as Jesus, but you are made in the image of God in moral, spiritual, and intellectual nature. All the goodness and fruit of the Spirit that you have inside of you is because you have the same Spirit of God inside of you.

It says in Romans 8:11, *"The Spirit of God, who raised Jesus from the dead, lives in you"* (NLT). You have the nature of God inside of you, which doesn't mean you do everything perfectly as He does, but it does mean you have those qualities and nature inside of you, and you can ask God to help you act out of your spirit rather than out of your flesh (your carnal nature).

So God created man in his own image, in the image of God he created him; male and female he created them. (Genesis 1:27)

And have put on the new self, which is being renewed in knowledge after the image of its creator. (Colossians 3:10)

My old self has been crucified with Christ. It is no longer I who live, but Christ lives in me. So I live in this earthly body by trusting in the Son of God, who loved me and gave himself for me. (Galatians 2:20 NLT)

You are REDEEMED—bought with Christ's blood, made whole, and restored from the curse of sin and death.

There are so many amazing parts about who we are in Christ, but this might be my personal favourite!

We were destined for a life of sin and debt, death and ruin, but because Jesus came and died on the cross, we have been set free from the law of sin and death! Because of Jesus' sacrifice, we no longer have to carry the burden of sin in our lives—we are set free! God bought us through the blood of Christ, and because of that, we no longer need to fear our future because we will be with Him in heaven for eternity!

God gave you a fresh start, and He continues to work in your life to sanctify you and make you clean. We are always a work in progress, but thankfully, God is always working in us! He doesn't quit or give up, no matter how many mistakes we make. Because of Christ's sacrifice, we inherit the blessing of redemption in our lives—it is yours!

For you know that God paid a ransom to save you from the empty life you inherited from your ancestors. And it was not paid with mere gold or silver, which lose their value. It was the precious blood of Christ, the sinless, spotless Lamb of God. (1 Peter 1:18–19 NLT)

He is so rich in kindness and grace that he purchased our freedom with the blood of his Son and forgave our sins. (Ephesians 1:7 NLT)
See also 1 Corinthians 6:20; Galatians 5:1; and 1 John 1:9.

You are CHOSEN—purposely picked out by God.

God chose you before the foundation of the earth (Ephesians 1:4). He knew that you were exactly the "you"

He had in mind when He created you. God chose us before time and creation, showing us that He chose us because He loves us, not because of our own work or merit.

> *You did not choose me, but I chose you and appointed you that you should go and bear fruit and that your fruit should abide, so that whatever you ask the Father in my name, he may give it to you. (John 15:16)*

> *But you are a chosen race, a royal priesthood, a holy nation, a people for his own possession, that you may proclaim the excellencies of him who called you out of darkness into his marvelous light. (1 Peter 2:9)*

> *Before I formed you in the womb I knew you, and before you were born I consecrated you; I appointed you a prophet to the nations. (Jeremiah 1:5)*

> *Blessed be the God and Father of our Lord Jesus Christ, who has blessed us in Christ with every spiritual blessing in the heavenly places, even as he chose us in him before the foundation of the world, that we should be holy and blameless before him. (Ephesians 1:3–4)*

> *For many are called, but few are chosen. (Matthew 22:14)*

You are LOVED—fully loved beyond what you can imagine, without condition.

To talk about this and do it justice would take a lifetime. How to express or explain how much God loves you would be impossible to convey with human words. But God's love for you began before you were born, and He loves you just as much now as He did then. We said it a few pages earlier, but it's worth repeating: He will never love you more than He does right now, and He will also never love you less than He does right now.

There is nothing you could do that would stop Him from loving you, and His love is big and complete and joyful. It's all the goodness of God wrapped up in His expression of care and goodness toward you. If you don't know how much God loves you, I recommend doing a study on God's love. Look up every verse you can find that talks about His love. You can use the internet or a Bible app or even an old-school Bible concordance. You may just learn something you didn't know before that helps you understand just how much He loves you and how every act of goodness in your life revolves around His love for you.

But God shows his love for us in that while we were still sinners, Christ died for us. (Romans 5:8)

For God so loved the world, that he gave his only Son, that whoever believes in him should not perish but have eternal life. (John 3:16)

So we have come to know and to believe the love that God has for us. God is love, and whoever abides in love abides in God, and God abides in him. (1 John 4:16)

No, in all these things we are more than conquerors through him who loved us. For I am sure that neither death nor life, nor angels nor rulers, nor things present nor things to come, nor powers, nor height nor depth, nor anything else in all creation, will be able to separate us from the love of God in Christ Jesus our Lord. (Romans 8:37–39)

See what kind of love the Father has given to us, that we should be called children of God; and so we are. The reason why the world does not know us is that it did not know him. (1 John 3:1)

You are WORTHY—He chose to die for you.

I think we often glaze over this truth as a simple phrase because we hear it so much as Christians, but stop for a moment and re-read that sentence. Someone—not only someone, but God's only Son—died for you. Jesus chose to actually be tortured and killed, not because He had to, but because He loves you. Can you imagine doing that for someone else? I can't even fathom the depth of love that it would take for me to volunteer to die for someone. And the beautiful thing is we inherit this blessing simply because we believe. We take that gift for granted, but let's take a moment to thank Him right now for what He did and try to remember His sacrifice that allows us to be forgiven.

For the wages of sin is death, but the free gift of God is eternal life in Christ Jesus our Lord. (Romans 6:23)

But God shows his love for us in that while we were still sinners, Christ died for us. (Romans 5:8)

For by grace you have been saved through faith. And this is not your own doing; it is the gift of God, not a result of works, so that no one may boast. (Ephesians 2:8–9)

You are FORGIVEN—made fully right with God because of your faith.

Because of His sacrifice, you now get to come boldly before the throne of grace (Hebrews 4:16) and accept His forgiveness for your sin. If we had lived in Old Testament times, before the New Covenant, we would know what a gift it would be to live in the New Covenant. If you read through Deuteronomy, Leviticus, or Numbers, you will see what painstaking effort it took to be righteous before God. Sacrifices, fasting, having a priest atone for your sin, and a strict diet, among other things. To fulfill the law was impossible and all failed. God made the way possible for us by sending His Son, who paid that atonement for our sins and allowed us to come to Him directly. We don't have to do anything but believe in Him and accept Him as our Saviour, and we inherit *all* the blessings of salvation and forgiveness! What a privilege that we not only get access to God through Jesus, but we are also forgiven because of what He did. He took on sin and the punishment, the weight of the sins of the world, all *for* you. That is your inheritance in Christ—what an immense gift it is!

Therefore, since we have been justified by faith, we have peace with God through our Lord Jesus Christ. Through him we have also obtained access by faith into this grace in which we stand, and we rejoice in hope of the glory of God. (Romans 5:1–2)

You see that a person is justified by works and not by faith alone. (James 2:24)

If then you have been raised with Christ, seek the things that are above, where Christ is, seated at the right hand of God. (Colossians 3:1)

Who was delivered up for our trespasses and raised for our justification. (Romans 4:25)

Or do you not know that the unrighteous will not inherit the kingdom of God? Do not be deceived: neither the sexually immoral, nor idolaters, nor adulterers, nor men who practice homosexuality, nor thieves, nor the greedy, nor drunkards, nor revilers, nor swindlers will inherit the kingdom of God. And such were some of you. But you were washed, you were sanctified, you were justified in the name of the Lord Jesus Christ and by the Spirit of our God. (1 Corinthians 6:9–11)

For by grace you have been saved through faith. And this is not your own doing; it is the gift of God, not a result of works, so that no one may boast. (Ephesians 2:8–9)

You are SECURED FOR ETERNITY—your destiny is decided for you, and it's so incredibly GOOD!

Heaven is our eternal home. The earth is just the place we pass through to get there. But as part of your inheritance in Christ, God has given you a permanent residence for all of eternity, and it's the best place imaginable. We are so blessed that God not only lives inside of us here on earth, but when we pass away, we get to go live with Him, finally face to face, for all eternity. That is such a solid security that we have in Him. Anyone who accepts Jesus as their Lord and Saviour has this beautiful blessing as their inheritance.

He will wipe away every tear from their eyes, and death shall be no more, neither shall there be mourning, nor crying, nor pain anymore, for the former things have passed away. (Revelation 21:4)

In my Father's house are many rooms. If it were not so, would I have told you that I go to prepare a place for you? (John 14:2)

But, as it is written, "What no eye has seen, nor ear heard, nor the heart of man imagined, what God has prepared for those who love him." (1 Corinthians 2:9)

But our citizenship is in heaven, and from it we await a Savior, the Lord Jesus Christ. (Philippians 3:20)

You are SET APART—uniquely different but in a good way.

You are set apart from the culture around you. We are made to be salt and light and to draw the unbelievers of the world to Christ by how we live and how we love God's children and creation. We don't have to live as the unbelievers do, but instead, we have access to all the beautiful gifts that the Lord bestows upon us as His children.

But know that the LORD has set apart the godly for himself; the LORD hears when I call to him. (Psalm 4:3)

But you are a chosen race, a royal priesthood, a holy nation, a people for his own possession, that you may proclaim the excellencies of him who called you out of darkness into his marvelous light. (1 Peter 2:9)

All of these beautiful blessings are yours in Christ, but they're more than that—they're your identity in Him. This is part of who you are because of what Christ did for you. When life changes around you, or you feel like a stranger in the culture we live in, know that you're not alone and that you were made for a purpose. You are valuable and worth so much to your Father.

FOUND IN HIM

As a child, I remember a time when I got lost. I was around six or seven, and our family had gone to a neighbouring town to do some shopping. While we were stopped at a shop, at some point, I wandered to a different part of the store. While I was looking around the shop, my parents and siblings had moved on and left the store, thinking I was in tow. A few minutes passed, and I went looking for my parents in the store and couldn't find them anywhere. I frantically ran out of the store, thinking I would see them on the street and be reunited. However, they were nowhere in sight. I began to run down the road, looking everywhere for them, but I couldn't find them. I was quite young, but something inside of me knew that if I was going to find them again, I had to go somewhere they were inevitably going to look. I realized I needed to run back to our family vehicle and wait for them because they would eventually show up there.

Thankfully, they showed up not long after, but to me, it felt like an eternity. I was so glad to be found and all the angst and worry that I had felt melted away, and I was so relieved.

Knowing who you are is like that. It's a feeling of being found, of knowing who you are, of knowing that you're safe, protected, and in the right place at the right time. It's knowing Who you belong to and being safe and secure in that. When you don't know who you are, it's much like a child lost in an unknown city. You're unsure of your surroundings, you feel aimless and lost, you don't know where to go or how to feel, and you carry around worry and angst.

Life is ever-changing. One thing you *can* count on is change. Circumstances change all the time, and if you believe your identity is in those things, your sense of worth can change based on your circumstances. But when you're rooted and grounded in who God made you, it doesn't change because God doesn't change—He is constant. Who He was since the beginning of time is who He is today. Isn't that incredibly comforting? What He says about *you* today is the same thing He said about you when He chose you, and He will say the same things about you when you're old and grey because you're His child; you're redeemed, loved, valuable, forgiven, chosen, and to Him, you're worth dying for. Those things won't change, regardless of whether the circumstances in your life change or not.

When you understand who God made you to be, your life can be so full of joy regardless of your circumstances. Your purpose is to live that out while loving God and loving His people. That's why your worth can't be found in your pant size, your hair, your stretch marks, or your wrinkles—because those things don't have anything to do with who you are. They don't define you—but God has. *Let the one who created you be the one who defines you.*

WHO YOU ARE in CHRIST

You are God's CHILD—first and foremost. You were an orphan, but you've been adopted by your Father.

You are VALUED—you are of utmost importance, and He takes great care in taking care of you.

You are made in GOD'S IMAGE—with all the attributes of a righteous heart.

You are REDEEMED—bought with Christ's blood, made whole, and restored from the curse of sin and death.

You are CHOSEN—purposely picked out by God.

You are LOVED—fully loved beyond what you can imagine, without condition.

You are WORTH DYING FOR—He chose to die for you.

You are FORGIVEN—made fully right with God because of your faith.

You are SECURED FOR ETERNITY—your destiny is decided for you, and it's so incredibly GOOD!

You are SET APART—uniquely different but in a good way.

CHAPTER SEVEN

A Love Letter

W hen my husband and I first began dating, geographically, we lived far apart from each other. He lived in Kamloops, and I lived in Duncan, on Vancouver Island. Our travel time between destinations was approximately twelve to fourteen hours. It involved waiting for a ferry, crossing the ocean, docking, driving or catching a bus through the mountains, and ending up in each other's respective cities. It was a huge commitment but also financially a struggle to see each other more regularly than once a month, being that we were so young when we met (sixteen and seventeen). Because of our geographical distance, we learned how to stay connected and in close relationship with each other even though we couldn't see each other. (Yes, this was well before FaceTime—can you imagine?) We talked on the phone, we wrote emails, and we sent each other messages on MSN chat (shout out to all my fellow millennials), but one of our favourite things to do was write each other letters. Physical letters. You know the ones? Paper, pen, envelope, and stamp? Yeah, those. It became a way to stay connected, but it was also a joy to get the mail and squeal with delight when a special surprise from the other person was hidden amongst the usual mail of bills. It brought an instant smile when we saw one of those envelopes.

Thankfully, we have kept all the letters we wrote to each other over the year that we dated long-distance. They are folded up in an old leather mini-backpack (yes, there are enough to fill a backpack!), and from time to time, we pull them out and reminisce about what was going on in our lives at that time, how we felt, or the kind words said to each other. It's an incredibly special blessing to have those letters because they give us something tangible to read, see, and remember about a very special time in our lives many years ago that brought us closer together. Without those letters, our love wouldn't change, but with those letters, we are able to recount things we wouldn't have remembered had we not had them.

God tells us, through the words of His servant David, that we are to recount the goodness of the Lord—to remember His works and remind ourselves of all the good that He has done (Psalm 77:10–20). Why? Because it builds our faith and reminds us of things we may have forgotten, such as past victories or stories of redemption and overcoming obstacles. In short, it builds our faith and hope in the good still to come and helps remind us of the truth when our faith is being tested through trials.

In the very same way, God has given us His Word, and His Word is like a love letter to us. He tells us the story of how we came to be, the story of our creation and downfall, and how He had great mercy on us time and time again. He tells us how He made a way for us and gave us eternal life beyond anything we could ever imagine. The story of history (or as I call it, His-story) is a love letter from God to His children, reminding us of who we are, how He saved us through His mercy, and the good things He has in store for us.

Just like my husband and I have those letters to look back on and remind us of times past, God wants to remind us of His love through His love letter—the Word of God.

The entire Bible is a love letter from our Father God to us, His children. But He has given us one love letter in particular that speaks specifically to who we are and how He sees us. That love letter is Psalm 139. It includes the smallest of details about how we were formed and what God thinks about us. It's an important passage, and we ought not to gloss over it but instead, ponder, pray through, and slowly digest it. This passage of Scripture can change how you see your relationship with God because it sheds such a different light on God's thoughts about us.

Let's read through the whole passage first, and then we

will break it down into more of a commentary on each
verse.

O LORD, you have examined my heart
  and know everything about me.
You know when I sit down or stand up.
  You know my thoughts even when I'm far away.
You see me when I travel
  and when I rest at home.
  You know everything I do.
You know what I am going to say
  even before I say it, LORD.
You go before me and follow me.
  You place your hand of blessing on my head.
Such knowledge is too wonderful for me,
  too great for me to understand!
I can never escape from your Spirit!
  I can never get away from your presence!
If I go up to heaven, you are there;
  if I go down to the grave, you are there.
If I ride the wings of the morning,
  if I dwell by the farthest oceans,
even there your hand will guide me,
  and your strength will support me.
I could ask the darkness to hide me
  and the light around me to become night—

but even in darkness I cannot hide from you.
To you the night shines as bright as day.
Darkness and light are the same to you.
You made all the delicate, inner parts of my body
and knit me together in my mother's womb.
Thank you for making me so wonderfully complex!
Your workmanship is marvelous—how well I know it.
You watched me as I was being formed in utter seclusion,
as I was woven together in the dark of the womb.
You saw me before I was born.
Every day of my life was recorded in your book.
Every moment was laid out
before a single day had passed.
How precious are your thoughts about me, O God.
They cannot be numbered!
I can't even count them;
they outnumber the grains of sand!
And when I wake up,
you are still with me! [. . .]
Search me, O God, and know my heart;
test me and know my anxious thoughts.
Point out anything in me that offends you,
and lead me along the path of everlasting life.
(Psalm 139:1–18, 23–24 NLT)

Let's discuss each verse in more detail.

v. 1: O LORD, you have examined my heart
   and know everything about me.

God knows you. To be fully known is an incredibly peaceful feeling. When you know that someone fully knows you, it gives you confidence that even your flaws are okay because you know that they've seen or know your flaws, yet they still love you anyway. It allows you to rest, fully. To be fully known is a gift that we can easily take for granted, but when we realize that God fully knows us—the good, the bad, and the ugly—we can rest in our relationship with Him because even in fully knowing all the parts of us, He still chooses us and still loves us without any condition attached. What a beautiful gift that is and a reminder from Him that He loves all the parts of you.

vv. 2–3: You know when I sit down or stand up.
   You know my thoughts even when I'm far away.
You see me when I travel
   and when I rest at home.
   You know everything I do.

God knows not only your heart, as we see in verse 1, but He also knows all that you do, day and night. He sees you working out, doing a kind gesture for a neighbour, sitting in chemotherapy treatment, or working hard at your job. He is with you when you're driving kids to practice or cleaning out the vehicle, and He is with you in all the things in-between. He knows the thoughts you have even before you think them, helping refine your thinking into a more godly perspective so you can live in more and more knowledge of the truth. He cares about every thought that crosses your mind because He cares about every single part of you. You're never alone because He loves to be with you wherever you are, all the time.

v. 4: You know what I am going to say even before I say it, LORD.

God knows everything there is to know about you. He knows your thoughts; He knows your past, your pain, the wounds you bear, the burdens you carry, and all the desires and thoughts of your heart. He knows you intimately. He knows you better than you know yourself. He knows you completely. There is nothing left out that He doesn't know. He knows your good thoughts and your sinful ones, He knows your strengths and your weaknesses, and He loves you regardless of the right or wrong you do. He knows you completely because He loves you and is intimately acquainted with every part of you. He knows all that about you, and He loves you in spite of all your failures and flaws. None of that changes how He feels about you. That is a God who is deeply in love with His children.

v. 5: You go before me and follow me.
You place your hand of blessing on my head.

God is with you wherever you go. When you're flying in an airplane, His presence is with you. When you're scared, alone, or hurt, God is there with you. When you're making wrong choices and feel like you can't do anything right, God is with you. No matter where you go, He is there. But He's not just there—His blessing and protection are upon you. You can never run away or leave His presence because His hand is upon you. He hedges you in before and behind, meaning He not only puts protection around you on every side, but He is the God of time and space, so He sets up what you need before you even know you need it. He is always ready and never surprised by the things you encounter. He knew it was coming, and He already has a plan in place, ready for you to walk out. You don't need to be afraid of the trial ahead; He's already provided for it.

v. 6: Such knowledge is too wonderful for me,
too great for me to understand!

We can't even begin to understand how God loves us and the good thoughts He has toward us. If we tried to understand or think about how God views us, we would get a mind cramp because His ways are so beyond our ways, and His thoughts so beyond ours. We can just rest in knowing that He loves us so deeply, and we can ask for revelation to understand that, but as humans, I don't believe we could ever fully understand because it's too big and amazing for us to fully comprehend. Knowing that gives me great joy because it's greater than I can imagine and what I imagine is so beautiful and makes me feel so deeply known and loved already.

vv. 7–10: I can never escape from your Spirit!
   I can never get away from your presence!
If I go up to heaven, you are there;
   if I go down to the grave, you are there.
If I ride the wings of the morning,
   if I dwell by the farthest oceans,
even there your hand will guide me,
   and your strength will support me.

Wherever we are, we are with God. He is an ever-present presence. He doesn't ever leave us, and you could do everything imaginable to try and escape God, but you can't. Even the biggest sinner in the world cannot escape God or His presence.

I'm sure you've heard amazing testimonies of people living a life of sin who have had a profound encounter with God even while doing crimes, or drunk, or on drugs. God's presence completely changed them and caused them to turn from their life of crime, repent, and be saved.

It's not just the unsaved who encounter God in big ways; it's all of us. When you're afraid or sad or in a tough situation, God is with you in it, and He will give you what you need to get through it—that is a promise from Him (1 Corinthians 10:13; Philippians 4:19). It doesn't depend on you to overcome it alone, but you can depend on God to help you through it. Isn't that an absolute gift, friend?

vv. 11–12: I could ask the darkness to hide me
  and the light around me to become night—
but even in darkness I cannot hide from you.
To you the night shines as bright as day.
  Darkness and light are the same to you.

We think that when we make a mistake or sin, God will be mad at us or hold it against us. We believe that if we make a mistake, surely God can't use us because He only uses the perfect, or at least someone better behaved than you. But there is a difference between wickedness and weakness. Wickedness is a choice to disobey God and to keep choosing that without repentance or redemption. But weakness is our flesh warring with our spirit. Our spirit knows what to do, but our flesh wars with it to win. Like Paul said in Romans 7:15–24:

> *I do not understand what I do. For what I want to do I do not do, but what I hate I do. And if I do what I do not want to do, I agree that the law is good. As it is, it is no longer I myself who do it, but it is sin living in me. For I know that good itself does not dwell in me, that is, in my*

sinful nature. For I have the desire to do what is good, but I cannot carry it out. For I do not do the good I want to do, but the evil I do not want to do—this I keep on doing. Now if I do what I do not want to do, it is no longer I who do it, but it is sin living in me that does it. So I find this law at work: Although I want to do good, evil is right there with me. For in my inner being I delight in God's law; but I see another law at work in me, waging war against the law of my mind and making me a prisoner of the law of sin at work within me. What a wretched man I am! Who will rescue me from this body that is subject to death? Thanks be to God, who delivers me through Jesus Christ our Lord! (NIV)

Even in our weaknesses and mistakes, God is still with us; He can still make the darkness into light when we give it to Him. He still breaks through our fleshly desires and shows us the way with His guiding light. Even in the midst of a completely dark room, one tiny spark of light can illuminate the darkness. It doesn't work the other way around: darkness cannot overtake a bright room. God is our light, and He can touch all the spaces that need His light to illuminate them. What He illuminates can then be dealt with and healed. No amount of darkness can overtake His light.

vv. 13–16: You made all the delicate, inner parts of my body

   and knit me together in my mother's womb.
Thank you for making me so wonderfully complex!
   Your workmanship is marvelous—how well I know it.
You watched me as I was being formed in utter seclusion,
   as I was woven together in the dark of the womb.
You saw me before I was born.

   Every day of my life was recorded in your book.
Every moment was laid out
   before a single day had passed.

This passage describes just how much detail and care God put into making you. You were not an accident or part of the process of the human experience that just happened to be born. You were actually picked and chosen by God. Can you wrap your head around that? He decided that the world needed someone like you—hand-picked, hand-crafted, made uniquely by Him.

At craft fairs, oftentimes, the price of goods is higher than at a retail store because the goods being sold are handmade—hand-painted, hand-stitched, hand-woven. The added work of the artist making their art with their hands rather than a machine gives it added value because it is often more durable, higher quality, and more detailed, thus, more valuable. An artist creating their art using their hands is the highest form of value in the world of art. When you compare that to how God created you, He says

He specifically created you with His own hands in your mother's womb. There is no higher form of care, attention, and love than this.

Verse 14 says that we are "wonderfully complex" because God's works are marvelous. God didn't just happen to make you as a quota to fill; He made you beautiful, precious, and wonderful in His sight.

As it says in verse 16, every single day of your life was prepared before you even took your first breath. The problem you're having with your co-worker that seems insurmountable? God knew. The diagnosis you got from your doctor? God was prepared. He knew the troubles and hardships that you would face, and He already had a plan in place for you.

He also knew all the good plans He made for you. The birth of your child that changed your life? He planned that. Enjoying that beautiful view from the top of the mountain you hiked up? He painted that sky just for you to enjoy. Hard things come our way from the enemy or just simply because of the reality of sin on the earth, but God knew it all and He already had a plan to overcome it. Our God is a God who gives such attention to detail and who loves to show His love to His children. He has such good plans for each day of your life, although sometimes we get too busy to stop and see it.

The next time you notice something good—even the really small stuff—stop and recognize that God is giving you a wink from Him to let you know He did that just for you, just because, and then thank Him for it. Thank Him for the small detail that made your morning. Thank Him for placing blessings in your path, big or small, that bring joy to your day.

v. 17–18a: How precious are your thoughts about me, O God.

They cannot be numbered!
I can't even count them;
they outnumber the grains of sand!

God not only thinks about you, He thinks *good* things about you. Just like in a new romantic relationship, you often daydream about the person regularly, daydream about your time with them, ponder all the ways you love them, think about how excited you are to see them next—all those things and more, our God thinks about you.

Sometimes, it's easy to imagine God being disappointed with us when we think about how much we mess up and make mistakes, but God doesn't think that way. He is disappointed when we choose sin over righteousness, but He doesn't hold that against us. Because of repentance, we are forgiven in His sight. God is proud of you, happy that you spend your time desiring to serve Him, and He's so in love with you.

Verse 17 says that His thoughts about us are precious, and they can't even be counted because they're so numerous. Imagine how many there must be if they outnumber the grains of sand on a beach. That's an incredibly large amount. Even more amazing is they're not dependent on your behaviour because God doesn't love you with condition; He loves you unconditionally because He *is* love.

As Christians, we desire to echo God's character in everything we do—be forgiving, be kind to others, etc. But it also includes thinking about ourselves the way God thinks about us. If God is thinking beautiful and good thoughts about you, then who are you to think badly of yourself? Who are you to tear down how you look, or dwell on what people think about you, or criticize your body, or think you're ugly because you believe you have too many freckles?

No, God models how we should live and act, and if His thoughts about us are good, then our thoughts about us should line up with how He thinks about us. We should love ourselves in a balanced way, not picking and tearing apart things about ourselves, such as our personality or appearance. After all, He knew exactly what He was doing when He created you, and He loves to think good things about you—you're His daughter. Don't waste your time thinking wrong things about yourself, but instead, love yourself the way that God loves you—not pridefully but accepting that if He can think good things about you, you can, too.

v. 18b: And when I wake up,
you are still with me!

I have always loved this line, which seems somewhat isolated but speaks precisely to the faithful character of our God. Even when we get down on ourselves, even when we feel alone, even when we feel we aren't doing anything right and keep messing things up, God is still with us! He is with us while we sleep and all throughout the day. We wake up to His new mercies every morning. He never leaves us, and His good thoughts about us never leave Him. He is always thinking about you, morning and night.

vv. 23–24: Search me, O God, and know my heart;
test me and know my anxious thoughts.
Point out anything in me that offends you,
and lead me along the path of everlasting life.

David ends the psalm with a challenge for himself. He doesn't want anger and bitterness in his own heart, even if he hates sin the way God does. He wants to have a clean heart toward not only God but his fellow man. To really honour and glorify God, David doesn't need to focus on hating the wicked but on loving them. He realizes his need for God to remove his sin, search his heart, and flush out the sin that lies even below the surface of his understanding.

After reading through the love letter of Psalm 139, I hope that the truth about who you are and how God sees you sinks into your heart and you feel it confirmed in your Spirit. I pray that it becomes a *revelation,* not just *information.* I pray that it is something you ponder and think about regularly. I pray that the words of the psalmist become deep truth in your realization of how God sees you.

CHAPTER EIGHT

Arise, Daughter

As a mother, I want better for my kids than I had. I want to see them live a life full of rich*er* experiences, deep*er* closeness with God, and great*er* opportunities than I had. I want to see them rise up into who they were created to be and live that out without fear or hesitation. I want to see them step into the full calling and destiny of who God created them to be, and I want to encourage and build them up in any way I can.

We—you and I—are God's daughters. We aren't just His friends or His workmanship, but we are called to something higher, more intimate: We are family. We are His children, His kinship, His beloved. He wants to see us step into our calling, step into our purpose, and do it without fear or trepidation. He wants us to laugh "*without fear of the future*" (Proverbs 31:25 NLT). This is God's *design* for us, His purpose for us, His plan for us. He hardwired something incredibly unique into the design of a woman: a tenderness of heart, a nurturing spirit, and a gentleness with those He's given us to take care of, and He designed us with that purpose in mind.

Truthfully, you will not walk into your God-ordained destiny if you're afraid of who you are. God cannot take you to the deeper places if you are unsure of your capacity. You have to be willing to leave the safety and comfort of the boat and take a step out onto the water before God will place you in the deep. It's only in the deep that we find out who we truly are. It's only in the deep that we see if our faith is walking on top of the waves or sinking beneath it. In the deep is where you're tested and tried to see what you truly believe, yet if you're constantly insecure or confused about taking that step of faith, you will never be able to withstand the scrutiny of the testing. You have to be solid and confident in who you are—in who God made you to be—otherwise, you'll always be questioning yourself and living the counterfeit version of yourself.

God is calling His daughters to step out of the boat and let go of the safety net—He's waiting for you to take your hand off the boat. I sense that God is calling us as women to stop being consumed with the things of this life that are fickle and don't matter. What matters is how we live out our faith. Are we making disciples? What matters is our children and their future, their faith, their walk with God, and their purpose on this earth. What matters is the hearts that are lost that need to be brought back to Christ. What matters is loving the unlovable, the difficult, the unseen, the lonely, and the insecure into new life rather than death. When we focus on the waves we are walking upon and let them overwhelm us, we lose sight of what God is doing.

BE BOLD AND COURAGEOUS

Do you remember the story of Jesus walking on water? Jesus invited Peter to come to Him on the water (Matthew 14:29). When Peter stepped out of the boat, he didn't step into calm waters; he stepped out into the storm. He didn't wait for the storm to end before he put his foot upon the waves. When Peter walked on water, he walked *above* the waves and into the wind. He was not affected by the storm because he walked above it. He wasn't shaken by the wind, the tossing waves, or the darkness of the sea because he had his eyes fixed on Jesus. It was as if he had laser focus directed only on Jesus, and when he did that, nothing about his circumstances bothered him. He had enough faith to believe that Jesus would help him do what he needed to do, and he stood above it all. Peter didn't wait for the storm to be gone before he walked out his faith, and similarly, we don't have to wait for the storms of life to be resolved before we take a step of faith.

But Peter had a moment of panic as soon as he realized what he was doing, as soon as the doubts crept in that he was doing something impossible by human standards, as soon as he took his eyes *off* of Jesus—that's when he sank because he stopped focusing on Jesus, and instead, focused on himself.

Peter is one of my favourite people of the New Testament because I think I'm a lot like Peter. Peter acted out of emotion at times, like when he sliced off the soldier's ear because he felt it was his duty to defend Jesus. I can be like that. I act out of my emotions at times, not acting in a godly way because my feelings are leading me rather than the Holy Spirit in those moments.

But also, like Peter, there are many times when I am filled with faith and step boldly out of the boat and onto the water. Sometimes, though, doubts from the enemy creep in, and I begin to question my choices. I let the enemy rob me of standing on faith and instead focus too much on my circumstances and ultimately sink. Like Peter, one moment I can be telling Jesus I want to go to the cross with Him, that I will not let Him bear it alone, then in the very next moment I'm denying knowing Him at all.

Peter exemplifies the man (or woman) who loves God and who desires to be bold and courageous but struggles with human nature getting in the way of walking it out with complete perfection. Yet, God loved Peter, regardless. In fact, when Jesus rose from the dead, Peter was the first disciple Jesus revealed Himself to. I believe He revealed

Himself to Peter first because He wanted him to know that even though Peter's flesh had prevailed and he had denied Jesus, Jesus loved him just the same as He always had because Peter was always *fully known*—and *fully loved.*

COUNTER-CULTURAL

We are living in dark and challenging times. We live in an age when everything that's true is being questioned: identity, gender, absolute truth, what's right and wrong, sexuality, and purpose, among other things. It's a time that's riddled with individual truth rather than absolute truth. It's a time in which money and physical beauty are elevated beyond their rightful places, and those things are more highly valued by the culture around us than things that are much more important, such as integrity, values, morals, righteousness, how we treat each other, peace, and many other things, but most of all, Jesus. The culture around us has lost sight of what's important, of what's valued by God, but we don't need to also lose sight of that as Christians.

Sometimes, we struggle as women of faith to rise above the cultural norms and stand strong with the sword of truth and the shield of faith. We struggle to live out our faith all the time as we ought to, and at times, we find ourselves mimicking the culture instead of changing the culture. We are content with blending in rather than standing out. We are afraid of being cancelled for standing up for our beliefs rather than standing strong in our convictions. If we shy away from speaking the truth, how will the lost know the way? There aren't multiple ways to God; there is only one way, but if we are content with blending in, what will make us stand out? How will they know we are Christians? How will they know they're lost unless we show the culture a way to be found?

Women are designed for community—to connect on a deeper level to other women. It's not a surprise that God made us *sisters* in Christ because His design for us was to uplift, encourage, contend, and pray for our sisters, not compete, speak poorly of, or compare ourselves to each other.

God created everything diversely because God loves uniqueness, yet at times, we are striving to fit in with the culture around us, trying to conform. "*Don't copy the behavior and customs of this world, but let God transform you into a new person by changing the way you think. Then you will learn to know God's will for you, which is good and pleasing and perfect*" (Romans 12:2 NLT). The Apostle Paul is reminding us that we are to stand out from the culture around us so that we will be different, with our minds in line with God's will, not the culture's, in hopes that through us, others will be led to Christ.

Standing out may seem scary, lonely, and counter-cultural. It can be uncomfortable at times, and we often don't like to get too far out of our comfort zone, so we opt to blend in instead. But there's no life or growth in that, and I, for one, am tired of playing it safe. I'm tired of us—as women of God—believing the lie of comparison that we need to be the same as someone else. I'm tired of us believing that we need to fit into or blend into the culture. I'm tired of us feeling pressure to be so passive that we need to be careful not to speak the truth too boldly, or we will offend someone. The truth needs to be spoken. We shouldn't be sitting idly by while the truth is being assaulted. We need to speak the truth but always in love. Love, after all, covers a multitude of sin (1 Peter 4:8).

It's time for us as women to begin speaking the truth of the gospel and applying it to our lives. The time is now for the daughters of the King to show the culture around us how we should love each other, how to walk in our calling—to show the culture around us which things should be valued instead of listening to what the culture around us says is valuable. We cannot sit comfortably in a culture of sin with our eyes closed and our mouths shut.

God loves His children, and the only way to share that love with the rest of the world who doesn't yet know Him is to start living it out, not just talk about doing it. Start forgiving. Stop being so easily offended. Start encouraging. Stop competing. Stop gossiping, and start speaking well of one another. If we don't begin walking these out in our personal lives, we are no longer leading by example but instead have become like the hypocritical Pharisees.

I believe that God's heart breaks for His daughters when they only see themselves as nothing more than a physical body, nothing more than an outer appearance to please others with—that they have nothing else to offer the world or those around them than a tight, thin body and a short skirt. God is calling out to His daughters to step into a new understanding—the truth—of who they are and Whose they are.

He's talking to those of you who live in a prison cell of unrealistic expectations about how you need to look on the outside. Those of you who don't know your true worth and value in Christ. Those of you who feel content to sit in the lifeless waters on the shore rather than plunge feet-first into the abundance of the deep. Those who are afraid rather than confident. Those who are stuck rather than moving. Those who are chained rather than free. This is not the life that God designed for His daughters. This is a prison cell that the enemy has created, and sadly, many women don't even know they're stuck in this prison cell because the enemy has disguised the cell to look like a palace.

He will distract you from what God's trying to show you; He will take your focus off learning who you are in Christ and instead tell you to seek the approval of others because theirs is the opinion that matters. He does this by making you believe that you need to fit a certain mold to be accepted by the culture around you or that you need to be or act or look a certain way to fit in. But daughters, you are children of the King. You are so much more than all those things. Take off the shackles and swing the prison door open because you're not a prisoner; God has given you the key out of that cell.

OUR LIGHT AND SHIELD

I *know* in my heart that God is calling you to more. I know because He's shown me His heart for His daughters and how the enemy has stolen that truth away. He's shown me how He sees you through His eyes and how the culture has tried time and time again to reduce women to nothing more than what they look like, nothing more than a shallow shell of what God has created.

You are so much more than just a body; you have gifts, talents, abilities, and beauty to share with those around you, but if you are content to focus only on the outside, those things will begin to fall away. And the less they're used, the harder they are to get back in use, much like a bike that's sat in the rain for a year, clunky and rusty—it doesn't run as smoothly as it used to. It can be restored, but it takes time, energy, and a set of tools to get it there. Much in the same way, you can begin to take back what the enemy has stolen from you, but it won't just happen on its own. The inheritance isn't gone, but it's been buried.

In Psalm 23, it says that God has prepared for us a lavish banquet table filled with all the best things we could ever imagine, yet we are content with sitting on the sideline, with nothing more than the few scraps we were able to scrounge from under the table.

What are you settling for? What mold are you trying to fit into that wasn't made for you? Are you trying to be something you're not? When we try to be something we aren't, we are struggling in our own human effort, which leaves us exhausted and always coming up short rather than embracing with confidence who God has created us to be. He can do in one second in His divinity what we could never do in a million years with our own struggle and effort. Think about that for a moment, and ask the Holy Spirit to show you where you've struggled to fit in by your own effort. Ask God what He would rather have you do. You will be so set free when you let go of striving and start accepting who He created you to be and instead learn your true identity—who God says you are. Ask Him, now, to tell you who you are, and listen to what He says.

Thankfully, God has given us His Word as a guide, which can help lead us into truth about many things in our lives. We have the privilege of knowing the absolute truth from His Word. It's the *one* thing we know to be 100 percent true. How incredibly amazing God's Word is. It's truly the *one* thing on earth that isn't tainted by sin or lies. Can you believe we have free access to it, as well as the beauty of what it can do for our lives? Look at what we know about God's Word and the life that proceeds from it:

For the word of God is living and active, sharper than any two-edged sword, piercing to the division of soul and of spirit, of joints and of marrow, and discerning the thoughts and intentions of the heart. (Hebrews 4:12)

But he answered, "It is written, 'Man shall not live by bread alone, but by every word that comes from the mouth of God.'" (Matthew 4:4)

Your word is a lamp to my feet and a light to my path. (Psalm 119:105)

In the beginning was the Word, and the Word was with God, and the Word was God. (John 1:1)

All Scripture is breathed out by God and profitable for teaching, for reproof, for correction, and for training in righteousness, that the man of God may be complete, equipped for every good work. (2 Timothy 3:16–17)

Sanctify them in the truth; your word is truth.(John 17:17)

Heaven and earth will pass away, but my words will not pass away. (Matthew 24:35)

But He said, "Blessed rather are those who hear the word of God and keep it!" (Luke 11:28)

Let the word of Christ dwell in you richly, teaching and admonishing one another in all wisdom, singing psalms and hymns and spiritual songs, with thankfulness in your hearts to God. (Colossians 3:16)

The grass withers, the flower fades, but the word of our God will stand forever. (Isaiah 40:8)

It is the Spirit who gives life; the flesh is no help at all. The words that I have spoken to you are spirit and life. (John 6:63)

Every word of God proves true; he is a shield to those who take refuge in him. (Proverbs 30:5)

So shall my word be that goes out from my mouth; it shall not return to me empty, but it shall accomplish that which I purpose, and shall succeed in the thing for which I sent it. (Isaiah 55:11)

I encourage you to go back and read those again, but really slow down and digest what each verse is saying.

The Word is living, active, and discerning the intentions of the heart. We live by the Word of God, not by carnal things of this world. It's a lamp to our feet and a light to our path; it's for training and correction. It is *truth;* everything will pass away except for God's Word. It is to dwell within us. It gives us life and spirit; it's a shield, and it won't return empty but will do what it accomplishes. This is just a tiny snippet of what we have through God's Word, and knowing this, we can believe what God says about us, Daughter.

Living in the world without deception would be amazing if it were possible. It would allow us to know *only* the truth and never believe a lie. It would look like us knowing our true identity without ever believing anything different. It would allow us to never question what we have in Christ. It would change culture. It would revolutionize the way we relate to each other and the way we see ourselves. I think we would see encouragement, forgiveness, friendship, community, and a bunch of women showing the love of God to one another.

This is God's design, His plan for His girls: to know Him first, to be filled up with the Holy Spirit, and to walk out our calling and purpose with love for one another. That starts with knowing your true identity in Christ and loving who God made you. Once you do that, it's so much easier to love everyone else.

It *is* possible, friends. We may live in a fallen world that's full of lies and deception, but we *also* have God's Word, and He gave it to us for purposes such as this: to learn and know who we are and to believe it wholeheartedly and live that out. When we live out our identity, we change lives. By living it out, we can affect real change in the lives of those around us and be salt and light to a very broken world.

We have to arm ourselves with the knowledge of Christ and the knowledge of *who* we are in Christ. We learn this by studying the Word and purposefully studying what God says about us. Armed with that knowledge and believing in that truth, God can use His daughters to build up and encourage a generation of women who will stand for truth and justice in a fallen and broken world. He will use His daughters to influence a generation of women from believing the lie that their value and worth are based on what they look like or what they do to believing they are who God says they are and, by doing so, set them free!

THE APPROVAL OF MAN

For am I now seeking the approval of man, or of God? Or am I trying to please man? If I were still trying to please man, I would not be a servant of Christ. (Galatians 1:10)

At times, I am the chief offender of this trap: seeking the approval of others. My aspiration for my own life is to live what Paul spoke about and walked out, to not rely on the approval of what others think but to only value what God thinks.

Seeking the approval of others is what leads to trying to change yourself to make others like you—which is not only exhausting but never leaves you content with who you are. It also steals your sense of worth because you feel you have to be someone else in order to be accepted. Behind that mask is a sneaky little lie that tells you that age-old lie from the garden: You're not enough. That lie sneaks up in many ways in our lives (we talked about some of these in chapter 4), but the more that lie bleeds into our minds, the less likely we are to see all the ways it dresses itself up.

The reason we need to break free from people pleasing or trying to gain people's approval is because staying in that mindset or pattern of behaviour will keep you trapped. It will stop you from walking in your identity and instead cause you to try to change who you are to cater to what people want—or what you think they want—in order to accept you. This leads to losing your identity. How can you be who you are and who God created you to be if you're trying to be someone that everyone likes? In order to be liked by everyone it means you'll have to cater to every single person's needs (because they're all different), all the while losing yourself and who you are.

Daughter, you are called to more!

A NEW IDENTITY IN CHRIST

Paul (before his conversion) went by the name Saul. He was a persecutor of Christians. He spent his days and nights torturing Christians, putting them in jail, and even sentencing them to death. He was misled, though, because he thought he was doing it in the name of God. He truly believed that what he was doing was ordained by God, because he wrongly believed that Christians were liars who were a threat to the Jewish religion. He was convinced that he was living out God's will for his life.

But then Jesus showed up.

When Jesus shows up, it changes *everything*.

Saul's eyes were opened, and God told him that what he was doing was wrong and that He wanted him to stop persecuting Christians and instead preach the good news of the gospel, which was indeed true! What a mindset shift that would have been!

Keep in mind, during this time, that would have seemed absolutely crazy. After all, Jews had a certain cache in that geographical location and era, and they had a bit of a mindset that they were better than those who weren't of the Jewish faith. Moreover, they definitely weren't to associate with Gentiles. Paul had a solid job persecuting Christians and was well respected for it among the Jews and Pharisees. To abandon all he knew and go and do what God was asking him to do would have seemed ludicrous to anyone—most of all Saul. Yet, encountering God is like that; logic goes out the window, and the Holy Spirit speaks such revelation to your heart that you can't un-see what you've seen, and it suddenly makes sense. Faith takes over. God bestows the gift of faith and helps you walk out what He's called you to.

When God called Saul to this new purpose in life, Saul began to be called by a new name, his Greek name, Paul, rather than his Hebrew name, Saul. There is a misconception with this passage among some Christians, who were told (by man, not by Scripture) that God changed his name, but that's not the case. After his conversion, he is still called Saul at times in Scripture, but gradually, we see him referred to only as Paul. It's worth noting that after his encounter with Jesus, he began referring to himself mostly by his Greek name. This shift illuminates the total transformation he went through— from a proud Hebrew and one of the religious elite to a missionary to the Gentiles. Referring to himself by his Greek name allowed him to witness to the Gentiles from a place of humility and familiarity rather than hierarchy. To me, this change in his name signifies the change that took place in his heart on that road to Damascus. I believe it also coincided with a recognition on his part of his new identity in Christ.

God was giving him his new vocational identity. No longer was he to live the way he was living before, act the way he was acting before, or do the vocation he was doing before. He was changed on that road to Damascus when he encountered Christ Jesus. Changing his name signified his newly realized identity in Christ.

Paul would have known that leaving his old vocation of persecuting Christians would be shameful and surprising to his peers. It wouldn't have made sense to anyone in his social, political, or spiritual circle, but he was more enthralled with living out what God was calling him to than he was about protecting his reputation. Had he only been concerned about his reputation, he says he would not now be an apostle of the Lord Christ: *"Am I now trying to win the approval of human beings, or of God? Or am I trying to please people? If I were still trying to please people, I would not be a servant of Christ"* (Galatians 1:10 NIV). He was willing to stand firm on who God said he was rather than what the culture said he should be. He stood firm in his identity, which meant that he couldn't cater to anyone's opinion of himself anymore. He stopped caring about the approval of man and only cared about the approval of one: God.

Would you be bold, like Paul, and ask God to rename you in the areas where you've allowed the fear or approval of man to dictate your life? What labels or masks have you put on that the culture or the enemy tried to make you wear? Has the enemy told you you're worthless? Has he whispered that your past will always dictate your future? Have you believed the lie that you're damaged goods or ugly? Have you heard that you're better than others and taken *that* on as your identity? Have you believed the lie that you need to look a certain way to be accepted? There is no shortage of ways that the enemy uses lies to make us believe our identity is anything other than what God says it is, and he doesn't always use degrading things to attack your identity. *Many* times, he will use the root of pride to make you believe the lies he's telling you. All these things are examples of walking in an identity of the culture rather than your identity as a daughter of the King.

Ask God now to reveal to you the masks or identities that have a) been put on by you, b) been put on by the culture, or c) have been put on by the people around you. Ask Him now to show you; He will. Then, bring those masks to God and ask Him to show you what He says about you. Ask Him to show you your true identity.

SPEAKING TRUTH TO THE LIES

My desire is that you learn to *love* who God made you. He doesn't make mistakes. Love who you are inside, and love who you are on the outside. Even if you believe you're fifty pounds overweight, love yourself whether you stay that size or not. Don't let something as menial as pounds change how you see what God has made.

You may think you're living in a body that's not meant for you, but friend, if you're here, then God has you here for a reason. You're here for a purpose and it's not just to fit into a swimsuit that wasn't made for your unique body, so you can pose on a beach in front of a bunch of people whose opinions don't matter.

Working on yourself might mean slowly working toward losing some weight to get healthy, or it might mean accepting the pounds as they are (especially if you're struggling with health issues that cause it), but whatever it is, know that your size isn't what defines you, God is. Your weight or looks aren't your identity—they're the least interesting thing about you, yet they're the thing we often obsess the most over. Time to step into the truth of who you are, time to throw off the old identity of Saul and walk in the new identity as Paul!

Your size doesn't disqualify you. Have you let the enemy make you believe that it does? I believed for many years that my size disqualified me from many things:

being taken seriously, being seen as beautiful, working in ministry, being loved and accepted by those around me. All of those—every single one—were lies. I'm an incredibly determined, hard-working woman, yet I felt like because of my size, I might be judged as being lazy. God taught me that even if someone did think that, they didn't know the truth about who I was, and because of my identity in Christ, I could rest in the fact that it didn't matter what they thought. Those were chains that held me captive to a belief that my outside qualified or disqualified my inside. Insecurity and the approval of man often go hand in hand.

Thoughts often pass through our minds at such a quick speed that we don't realize how quickly we can scroll through the thoughts. That's why sometimes it takes a minute to catch ourselves. But each time I listened to those lies, not only did they not build me up, but they *always* tore me down. It may have started with tearing myself down about my appearance, but it didn't take long until that snowballed into other areas of my life.

I began second-guessing myself with decisions I was making. I started questioning relationships that I previously believed were solid. I began wondering where my worth was and seeking it in work or my roles as mother, wife, etc. I had opened the door for the enemy to lie to me in other areas. It was only once I realized I had allowed that that I began standing on the truth of God's

Word, no matter how much it conflicted with how I felt. And believe me, it was hard to believe something different than what I felt. I had to learn to replace those feelings—my dissatisfaction with my appearance—with the truth of who God says I am. Once I began doing that, I began to more quickly recognize the lies and cast them down immediately.

PEOPLE PLEASING

I'm not saying I'm never challenged to go back to the old way of thinking—that is always a possibility. I am challenged some days—some moments—but the difference now is I know the path to choose. I know the way out. This truth is beyond just knowledge; it's revelatory to me. I know that who God made me matters more than what the world says I should be.

Once you overcome on old thought pattern and learn a new way of thinking, it's fair to say you will still be challenged to revert back to your old way of thinking. You'll still be tested. You'll still be tempted by the enemy to see if you really believe what you say you believe. You'll still be questioned. And you'll still have to choose every time. Questioning the old way of thinking doesn't just magically go away because you chose it once. You'll need it choose it *every* time.

We make choices every day that may be in contrast to our feelings, but we choose them anyway. Just like you choose your marriage every day—even though some days are hard. Just like you choose to work out—even though you don't always feel like strapping on the shoes and heading out to get your sweat on. Just like you choose to make good choices with what you watch, what you eat, when you forgive someone who's hurt you—all the things you choose every day are because you know they're good for you or right, not because you necessarily feel like it.

This, dear friend, is no different.

You will be tested—to see if what you've learned can be put into practice, if what you've been taught is what you truly believe! You will be tempted by Satan to revert to old patterns because it's in the testing that we see what we truly believe. Do we believe God's approval is enough? Are we still looking for our worth in the things of the world? You won't always pass. Friend, if you fail the test, don't beat yourself up. Instead, shake the dust off your feet (Matthew 10:14) and try again, but this time, not in your own strength—draw on God's. He says His grace is sufficient for you. He says His power is made perfect in your *weakness*. Push forward and trust that God will continue to help you grow. He will. You'll get there.

I have an opportunity to be tested every time we go on a tropical vacation. There isn't a dress code in resorts, and going to the beach can feel like going to a burlesque show. Many women at the pool, restaurant, and beach often show most of their bodies, even their private areas, seemingly with no regard for how that may make anyone else feel. It's not fair to all the men on the beach who don't want to see that, and in the past, it's been a struggle for me to be around that scene and not feel insecure in my own skin.

But God is so incredibly gracious, and He has been working on me for a purpose. He's completed an incredible work in me (Philippians 1:6). Recently, we took a trip to Mexico for ten days. It was a beautiful time with our family. For the first time, I wasn't on edge about how I would feel seeing that familiar scene. I was the most at peace I've ever been. I didn't compare myself once. I didn't feel ashamed of my cellulite or my size. I didn't live in a parka, all covered up. I wore my full-piece swimsuit with confidence that I was exactly who God made me.

As for the other women who chose to dress inappropriately? That's their journey. That's not for me to judge or know why they chose to dress that way. *It's not my purpose to question theirs*. It's not my job to judge or criticize them or even to feel belittled by them. We never know what people are walking around with inside—pain or their own battle with insecurity—and we aren't meant to. We are meant to stay focused on the task ahead of us, our journey, our walk with God. My job—and my joy—is to be confident in who I am and who God made me and enjoy the blessing of the time I get to spend with my family in a geographically-stunning place that God created, fully enjoying all the splendour of His artistry.

In overcoming the approval of man, God highlighted places where I allowed others' opinions to outweigh God's in other areas beyond my appearance. Lies are like poison that slowly make their way through the veins, and they begin to affect every part of our lives.

Tearing yourself down, even unintentionally, is incredibly damaging to your soul and mind. God does not want us to be wimpy Christians who don't know what the truth is or who question our inner voice (the Holy Spirit). It says in Matthew 5:37, "*All you need to say is simply 'Yes' or 'No'; anything beyond this comes from the evil one*" (NIV). The enemy is the author of indecision, not God.

Jesus also says in John 10:27 that *"My sheep hear my voice."* This means we should be solid in our decisions and conviction leading from the heart because that's what we sense God leading us to do. Be confident in what God says about you. Trust that *still, small voice* inside. Hearing from God is our inheritance as daughters. Allow yourself the grace to hear from God, and trust that He will lead you.

Tearing yourself down leads to projecting that behaviour onto others. If you pick apart your looks, it's easy to believe that others do as well. If you think you have flabby thighs or thick ankles that everyone notices and is judging you for, you will believe that everyone notices and judges them, too, even if it's the last thing on anyone's mind. We project onto others what we think about ourselves, which is why it's so important to be grounded in the truth of who God says we are. It's also easier to pick other people's appearance apart because you're insecure about your own looks. This is a trap that is very easy to get into and very hard to get out of.

I believe perspective is important, and one thing the culture has done is unfairly idolized the external body, that it should be used to glorify ourselves rather than glorify God. We need to remember that our body is a temple but not meant to be an idol. How often we reverse the two.

Let's look at what Jesus says about how we should view our bodies:

If you decide for God, living a life of God-worship, it follows that you don't fuss about what's on the table at mealtimes or whether the clothes in your closet are in fashion. There is far more to your life than the food you put in your stomach, more to your outer appearance than the clothes you hang on your body. Look at the birds, free and unfettered, not tied down to a job description, careless in the care of God. And you count far more to him than birds. Has anyone by fussing in front of the mirror ever gotten taller by so much as an inch? All this time and money wasted on fashion—do you think it makes that much difference? Instead of looking at the fashions, walk out into the fields and look at the wildflowers. They never primp or shop, but have you ever seen color and design quite like it? The ten best-dressed men and women in the country look shabby alongside them. If God gives such attention to the appearance of wildflowers—most of which are never even seen—don't you think he'll attend to you, take pride in you, do his best for you? What I'm trying to do here is to get you to relax, to not be so preoccupied with getting, so you can respond to God's giving. People who don't know God and the way he works fuss over these things, but you know both God and how he works. Steep your life in God-reality, God-initiative, God-provisions. Don't worry about missing out. You'll find all your everyday human concerns will be met. Give your entire attention to what God is doing right now, and don't get worked up about what may or may not happen tomorrow. God will help you deal with whatever hard things come up when the time comes. (Matthew 6:25–34 MSG)

Or do you not know that your body is a temple of the Holy Spirit within you, whom you have from God? You are not your own, for you were bought with a price. So glorify God in your body. (1 Corinthians 6:19–20)

Our bodies are temples, not idols. They are containers for the soul and spirit, but their designed purpose isn't to glorify ourselves or man, but to glorify God. Being a certain size or look isn't what God cares about, nor does it glorify Him.

I appeal to you therefore, brothers, by the mercies of God, to present your bodies as a living sacrifice, holy and acceptable to God, which is your spiritual worship. (Romans 12:1)

Not only are our bodies temples, but when we submit our bodies to God, they are part of our worship to Him. This is one of those mysteries where God intertwines our physical bodies and our spiritual worship. We are not *just* physical or *just* spiritual. He put our soul inside a physical body, and He calls us to serve Him with those bodies. God is so amazing!

So, whether you eat or drink, or whatever you do, do all to the glory of God. (1 Corinthians 10:31)

We should not be gluttons or make food or our bodies an idol. Our bodies are necessary vessels for our spirits and minds, but how often they've been glorified as only serving the purpose of pleasing the eye and glorying one's self above another.

But I discipline my body and keep it under control, lest after preaching to others I myself should be disqualified. (1 Corinthians 9:27)

For you formed my inward parts; you knitted me together in my mother's womb. I praise you, for I am fearfully and wonderfully made. Wonderful are your works; my soul knows it very well. My frame was not hidden from you, when I was being made in secret, intricately woven in the depths of the earth. Your eyes saw my unformed substance; in your book were written, every one of them, the days that were formed for me, when as yet there was none of them. How precious to me are your thoughts, O God! How vast is the sum of them! (Psalm 139:13–18)

These are just a few references in God's Word as to how we should view the role of our bodies in this world. How often we give our bodies too much importance, and mental and emotional space, sometimes idolizing them without realizing it. It's understandable why it's hard to always recognize the lies that we need to look a certain way, because we live in a culture that idolizes physical appearance, but God's Word has the amazing ability to cut through the lies and tell us truth (Hebrews 4:12), and truth gives us *perspective* and knowledge. In this case, it teaches us the truth on the purposes and intentions of our bodies.

You may be saying to yourself, "That's great. Knowledge and truth are powerful, but what do I do with that knowledge? How do I apply that to my life?"

There are some practical ways you can apply this knowledge to your life. Practice these mindsets below:

• Keep these truths in focus and remind yourself of them if you get off track in your thinking or start tearing yourself down in any way: physically, making mistakes, etc.

• Knowledge helps us understand and do better. But also make this a prayer as part of your regular prayer life. Ask God to help you take this beyond knowledge, to a heart and mind revelation by the Holy Spirit. Don't stop praying if you don't see immediate results.

Changing mindsets takes time, but keep praying and keep believing.

• If you catch yourself seeking others' approval or validation, recognize what you are doing, and go back to reminding yourself of the truth above (keep the verses handy to read on your phone or printed and hung around your home). Change the script in your mind and continually remind yourself again of the truth. It will change your mind over time as you continue to repeat it.

• Practice the principles from page 125: Recognize, Reject, and Realign.

Armed with knowledge, the truth of God's Word, and the Holy Spirit working in your life, you really can begin to change the narrative in your mind.

Above all, remember that God made you a woman of God, able to fight the powers and principalities at work because God has already given you what you need, and He is always fighting your battles right alongside you with great power and all authority. Remember always, dear friend, that you were created for this time and place, to arise, Daughter.

CHAPTER NINE

Discipline

Have you ever trained for something? A race, an event, a contest, a performance on stage, etc.? I would argue most people have had to train for something at some point in their life, even if it was something as simple as a Christmas concert or practicing for a spelling test in school—each requires training!

Training for something takes a lot of things: time, energy, determination, and, most of all, discipline. Anyone who's trained for a marathon knows that a lot of work goes into the marathon long before the marathon even starts. You need to carefully monitor your food intake, develop a regimen of high-intensity physical training, and get the essential amount of sleep—the list of things you need to add to your routine or avoid is endless. But there's a purpose behind it: *Preparation leads to success.* If you were to neglect all those things and show up untrained to a marathon, the odds of you finishing the race or even making it halfway through would be slim to none. It's because we know that there are certain things that need to happen in order to be successful. However, it's even more than that. In order to be successful, you need to have discipline to do the things you need to do to get there. Without discipline, there will be no follow-through, only good intentions. Discipline is the decision you make to do something whether you *feel* like doing it or not—it's the *choice that precedes the outcome.*

It's funny how we celebrate discipline as a society when it comes to something like a marathon or the Olympics, yet, when it comes to disciplining our minds, we suddenly lose interest or think it doesn't seem as necessary or important.

Let me dissuade you of that notion right now.

Discipline is imperative to your life—mentally, emotionally, and spiritually. Discipline doesn't sound fun, and it's even less fun at times when you're in the middle of it, but the fruit that it yields makes it well worth the pruning.

You might have arrived where you're at because of some pain or trauma in your past, or you may be facing painful circumstances right now. It can be easy to get swept up in a sea of "*laters*" and "*at some points.*" It's even harder to be motivated when you're going through something hard, but that's exactly when discipline is most effective in producing good results.

As we talked about in chapter 3, we are not just a physical body. We are made up of a three-part system: body, mind, and spirit. We cannot separate one of those things from the other two because they're all equally a part of who we are and how we were made—all three parts work in sync.

We've talked in length throughout the entirety of this book about the importance of learning who God is, learning who God made you, and discovering who you are in Him. These principles will really help you grow in your relationship with God, and in turn, will allow you to draw nearer to Him. These are *spiritual disciplines*.

Making your *spiritual life* the *first* priority is imperative to your success. Without that, you will struggle to do any of the other things we are going to discuss. You walk the other disciplines out by partnering with God, but you have to build strength in your relationship with Him before you begin to tackle anything else. God has to be first: in your time with Him and going to Him in prayer. If you don't put God first in your life, everything else will be out of your own human struggle and effort. Please hear me loud and clear on this point—your spiritual life, your time with God, your intimacy with Him, knowing who He is, and being in His presence, that's the most important part. It will help sustain you in the other two areas: body and mind.

As we also talked about in chapter 3, we are not

strictly spiritual beings. We do, in fact, have a body and mind, as well. Our body and mind are important parts that help us function fully. If our body and mind are not properly taken care of, we will not function well in *any* of the three areas. They all work together in harmony with one another.

Being that we are not exclusively spiritual beings, there are some disciplines that need to be incorporated into your carnal life that will help you in many ways: physically, mentally, and spiritually. They all work in conjunction with each other to bring out the best in each area.

When you think of discipline, there are likely a few word associations that pop into your mind: boring, hard, frustrating, restricting, unfair, etc. Those may be your past associations with discipline, but if they *continue* to be your associations going forward, you're unlikely to reap the benefits of what we're talking about. Instead, I want you to associate discipline with success, pathway to freedom, and mental/emotional exercise—see it as a gift.

Discipline is necessary in our lives, despite what the culture around you may try to make you believe. Discipline is definitely counter-cultural. There's so much out there now about flexible lifestyles, the eternal vacation, that work is bad and play is good, that you should be able to eat all the things that make you feel good all the time, or that you should just do what feels good, in the moment, whenever you want. This is a dangerous mindset.

Our entire diet, media, and culture are consumed by this notion. Those things, in moderation, *are* good things. Vacations are a time to rest and take a break from the stressors of life. Delicious foods and treats are a lovely addition to life once in a while. Enjoying a laid-back Saturday with no schedule and nothing to do is a much-needed break sometimes—but it's not meant to be a way of life.

Anytime we only allow the fun things in life and try to avoid anything hard or anything that seems like work, we start to lose perspective and drive. We lose the perspective that fun comes with work, that joy comes with pain, and that treats come when you've been nourishing your body with nutrition, too. When we have a "party all the time" attitude, we lose sight of the importance of the other aspects of the realities of life. Without work, we wouldn't enjoy play because we wouldn't know what one felt like without the other.

All easy, all the time, is the stealer of true joy and the stealer of discipline. We are losing out on the joy of accomplishing something hard when we try to bypass the hardship.

We've talked at length about the importance of spiritual discipline throughout the book and built a strong foundation on God's Word. Let's take the time now to talk about the other two areas we haven't yet covered in the book in relation to discipline: body and mind.

BODY: ONE OF THE THREE PARTS

Disclaimer: As we talk about the body, I have no intention to cause shame of any kind. I hope you know that by now, dear friend! You are not defined by your body! But God did put us in physical bodies, and there are disciplines we can practice to take good care of those bodies and steward His gift as best we can.

Our bodies need certain things to function well. There's just no two ways about that. Our bodies need adequate sleep, proper nutrition, and activity and movement. Sometimes, however, we let those things get out of balance in our lives for different reasons: stress, a busy season, past traumas, and the list goes on. Our bodies will forgive us for a time, but our goal should be to try and get back into a good rhythm. We can struggle in other areas (mentally or spiritually) when we aren't taking proper care of our bodies.

We are going to look at a few important disciplines and how they relate to our physical body and its needs.

Food

Food is meant to fulfill our nutritional needs and properly

fuel our bodies. It absolutely can and should also be enjoyed, but its main function is not to necessarily just fulfill unhealthy cravings or make you feel good.

If you are eating only to make yourself feel good, there might be some emotional pain or issues at play. It's important to recognize if this is a pattern in your life. If you simply cannot stop yourself from overeating or binging on unhealthy food, you will need to dive into the issues behind that. Or it might be as simple as you've gotten yourself into a habit of eating for pleasure or boredom. Whatever the reason, pray and ask God to show you if this is an area you struggle in, surrender it to Him, and ask Him to help you.

We should, at our core, want to eat things that make our bodies strong and healthy. Substitutes for junk food, like sugar-free alternatives, can be used in moderation, but we should not aim to always eat foods that satisfy cravings. Often, those things come highly processed and aren't good for us.

Our bodies do crave fat, salt, and sugar—that's just part of our human makeup, often craving it more when we are stressed. Those are inherent in our cravings; however, we can learn to adopt incorporating healthy food through practice and discipline.

Being wise with what you eat does not mean you can't have the occasional cookie or treat here and there, but you do need to keep your treats in balance.

Ultimately, giving in to cravings all the time will never fully satisfy you—only God can. You're fooling yourself if you think food will ever satisfy you. Yes, we do get a hit of dopamine (a natural, feel-good hormone in our body) when we eat something that is delicious to us, and it reinforces that feeling, but we shouldn't ever let anything replace the joy and peace we get from God. Feelings are temporary, but the true joy we get from God is sustaining.

Fasting from food cravings and instead turning to God in prayer when you feel the craving come upon you can be an incredibly beautiful and intimate time with God. Fasting is a subject we aren't covering in this book, but I strongly recommend learning about it. *A Hunger For God,* by John Piper, is a good resource.

There's something powerful that is restored in us when we submit our cravings and fleshly desires to God. Consider fasting from those treat foods for thirty days, and when you feel tempted to give in, use that time to pray instead. You may be surprised not only by how much of a hold that food had on you but also what a bondage it can break when you submit yourself to God.

We need to be disciplined in how we use food in our lives, not as a substitute for happiness but as something we use to fill our hunger needs and nutritionally benefit us.

I am not, however, talking about eliminating food to lose weight or subscribing to a diet culture, which is another topic entirely—that is not the purpose. What I'm talking about is building intimacy with God and surrendering things that may be hindering your freedom.

Diet culture seemed to be rampant when I was growing up, and I've had to unlearn much of the messaging that was taught during that time. Although I didn't diet, it seemed that everyone around me did, and it really skewed the way I saw food. I saw women punish their bodies to make themselves feel prettier. How confusing for a young girl to make sense of it all.

Here is where I stand in respect to the role of food in my life: I respect that food is made by God for us and that our bodies know how to use it.

The goal here is to eat nutritiously to help nourish your body, but not become meticulous in micromanaging what you eat. Be wise, use good judgment, and don't abuse food. Abusing food would be things like only eating foods that satisfy unhealthy cravings, for example, eating a regular diet of pop, chips, candy, pastries, etc. Those things in moderation can be enjoyed from time to time, but in excess, they can make you feel crummy, and they will not contribute to good health. Be wise in your food choices, but don't make food an idol either way—by eating too much or restricting too little. Have balance!

A disciplined person who doesn't eat based on their feelings is someone who can be proud of the choices they make, which helps contribute to their mental health as well. Be disciplined by having balance.

Choosing Discipline

Choosing discipline is not typically the fun choice. I have definitely had seasons in my life when I've been more disciplined with my choices and seasons when I've really struggled to have discipline in different areas. Sometimes, life's circumstances, especially in stressful times, can lead to wanting to eat emotionally, skip your exercise routine, or stay up late. Sometimes, discipline seems boring or hard, and you want to give in. And once in a while, you can, but the habit should be formed in your life to choose discipline 85–90 percent of the time. You will feel good later for the choices you make now.

The same can be said for simple things like getting enough sleep, drinking enough water, and moving your body enough. Those things are good for you because they help you live a balanced life. Things like drinking enough water, sleeping enough, and getting enough movement in your life aren't necessarily fun things, but they contribute to a disciplined mind and body, and they contribute to taking good care of your body.

Scripture supports this notion of discipline: *"No discipline seems pleasant at the time, but painful. Later on, however, it produces a harvest of righteousness and peace for those who have been trained by it. Therefore, strengthen your feeble arms and weak knees"* (Hebrews 12:11–12 NIV). Paul is reminding us that the things that are important, the things that bring fruit in your life, and the things that are worth fighting for, often come with discipline. He could be talking about physical, spiritual, or emotional discipline here because they all work in conjunction with one another. Life isn't only about having fun; it's about being wise with the choices we make because choices are what lead you down either a fruitful path or a destructive one. It's important to recognize (as Paul pointed out) that discipline doesn't feel good "at the time," but later, it will produce a fruitful harvest in your life.

Paul also says: *"Do you not know that your bodies are temples of the Holy Spirit, who is in you, whom you have received from God? You are not your own; you were bought at a price. Therefore honor God with your bodies"* (1 Corinthians 6:19–20 NIV).

Our body is a temple, like we talked about in the last chapter. Paul is talking about respecting the body God gave you and treating it well in all areas because it's the home of God. God has given us these bodies, and we need to treat them as He designed—a holy temple for the Holy Spirit.

1 Kings 8 talks about the importance of the physical temple of God. Before Jesus came, while the Old

Testament laws were still in operation, the Israelites needed a place to worship God and bring their offerings and sacrifices. They had a physical temple to do that. The temple was meticulously built, and adorned with precious gold and jewels. It was a very treasured place—a holy place. It was where they went to convene with God.

When Jesus came, the need for a physical temple as a place to pray, worship, offer sacrifice for sin, and talk to God was no longer needed because the Holy Spirit came to live inside of us—*we* became the temple. In the same way that the temple for the Israelites was holy, we are to make our bodies holy. Part of taking care of our bodies is giving our body proper fuel (food), exercising, and filling our minds with good and godly things.

THE MIND

Along with taking care of our bodies (the temple), we also need to take care of our minds. We have talked throughout the book about our thoughts, but discipline also needs to be exercised in the mind.

There are two areas that we need to pay attention to when talking about mental and emotional health: the importance of what we put in (stimulus/input for our mind) and what and how we think (what we focus our mind on).

We would never physically consume a diet of garbage

(rotten food, plastic, cardboard) and expect our body to feel good—it would be detrimental to our health. In the same way, we cannot consume garbage for our mind all day and expect that our minds will be healthy.

A healthy mind needs a few things to help it run smoothly: a healthy physical body, a healthy spirit, and a discerning heart that uses wisdom regarding what you put into it. That means what we consume (mentally) can affect our health. That includes the kinds of shows we watch on TV, the things we read about online, the kinds of influences on social media, what we talk about with our friends, and the negative things we think about or dwell on. All of those things can negatively affect the health of your mind.

It's not just the health of your mind that's important, though; it's also the discipline of your mind. We know it's not healthy for children to be wild and free without rules or consequences. The same principle is true for our minds —they need healthy borders and boundaries.

As you begin praying and asking God about this, which I encourage you to do, be attentive and listen for that still, small voice that guides you while you're going about your day. God might be reminding you to keep your mouth quiet when you feel like sharing a juicy piece of gossip. Or He may nudge you to turn the TV off and instead take some time to pray. Or maybe you will suddenly sense that the show you're watching isn't good content to fill your mind with. It might be that feeling that keeps popping into your mind that what you're looking at or being fed on social media isn't good for you, and you feel compelled to take a break or cut it all together. (I'm not a big believer in social media myself, but that's a topic for another day.) It might be God reminding you of the things you should be thankful for rather than focusing on the negative. Those nudges are there, but they're quiet; you won't hear them if you aren't paying attention.

It's likely that hearing from the Holy Spirit won't be big or loud; it'll be a quiet nudging in your heart (1 Kings 19:12–13). The more you pay attention to it, the more you'll notice it, but you need to be attentive to that nudge. Don't toss it off as your own ideas, but instead pay attention to what you're thinking about. Slowly but surely, you'll begin to notice when the Holy Spirit is nudging you to make better choices or put disciplines in place about what you're feeding your mind.

Remember: Discipline is hard at the time, but the rewards are great.

Dr. Fabiola Riobé is an accomplished international executive, industry expert, and educational advocate passionate about promoting entrepreneurship and social impact. She writes in her article, "Discipline Pays Off: The Pain of Discipline Versus the Pain of Regret":

In life, we often face difficult choices that require us to choose between short-term discomfort and long-term benefits. One of the most common choices we face is embracing the pain of discipline or suffering the pain of regret.

The pain of discipline is the temporary discomfort we experience when we are working hard towards achieving our goals. It requires us to make sacrifices, develop good habits, and push ourselves to new limits. However, the reward for our discipline is that we enjoy the benefits of our hard work in the future. These benefits include financial stability, career growth, and personal development.

On the other hand, the pain of regret is the long-term suffering we experience when we fail to take action toward our goals. It is a chronic pain that never goes away, haunting us with thoughts of what could have been. We regret not taking the time to develop good habits or not pushing ourselves to achieve our full potential.

The truth is that discipline pays off. Sticking to a routine or pushing ourselves beyond our limits may be challenging, but the benefits are worth it. When we discipline ourselves, we create a foundation for success that can last a lifetime. We set ourselves up for a life free of the pain of regret, knowing that we did everything we could to achieve our goals.[11]

These are your choices, and there are only two: discipline with short-term pain resulting in long-term gain *or* the pain of regret, which is short-term happiness but long-term pain.

It says in 2 Timothy 1:7, *"For God did not give us a spirit of timidity or cowardice or fear, but [He has given us a spirit] of power and of love and of sound judgment and personal discipline [abilities that result in a calm, well-balanced mind and self-control]"* (AMP). I really like what the Amplified Bible points out in this verse. Not only has God not given us a spirit of fear, but He's given us power, love, sound judgment, personal discipline, and a well-balanced mind that has self-control. Can you comprehend the beauty and blessing in that list? That is *huge*—if we accept that truth and agree with it in our minds. God has *given* us what we need to be disciplined and make that discipline a part of our lives. Self-control and discipline are intertwined and are keys to success. An undisciplined person is a person who's led by their emotions and who lives without working toward goals and receiving the joy of their success.

Thankfully, we aren't doing this alone because God has given us the Holy Spirit. That's where the quiet nudging comes in. Notice and pay attention to the times you sense in your heart that you should make a better choice. I find the Holy Spirit will nudge me in practical things throughout my day, which helps me learn and do better. It might be new disciplines, new ways to look at situations, getting rid of something that isn't serving me well anymore—it can be anything!

From what we read in Scripture, we don't need to wonder if we have self-discipline (also called self-control); we do. We just read it above in 2 Timothy 1:7 that God has given us self-control. And Galatians 5:23 tells us that it's one of the fruits of the Spirit, meaning because the Spirit lives in us, we receive the characteristics of Jesus.

We see that Scripture plainly tells us that we have self-control (self-discipline), but it's a question of whether or not we're using or exercising it. I can't count the number of times I've heard someone say, "Oh, I can't do that; I have no willpower!" You do have it inside of you, but it's also true that we only use what we believe we have. If you believe you have no willpower, you will exhibit that behaviour, but if you instead believe the Scripture and what God says you have, you can accept that as truth and begin walking that out, regardless of your feelings. Reject the notion that you have no self-discipline. Believe that you do and start exercising it—because it's there!

Discipline is a muscle, meaning that it gets weaker or

stronger based on use. It will always be there, but if you stop using it, it will become weak. However, the good news is the more you use it, the stronger it will become!

ACCOUNTABILITY

If you're just beginning to exercise this muscle and you find you need some help using it, consider an accountability partner in the area you're working on. This will be a tool you can use to help keep you on track to stick to the goals you've set for yourself. It can be in the area of spiritual discipline, such as reading your Bible everyday, physical discipline, such as working out three times a week, or mental discipline, such as abstaining from a TV show you know you need to give up. Whatever the area, having an accountability partner can be helpful to get started or keep you on the right track. It can be anyone (family, friend, spouse, pastor, etc.), but it needs to be someone you trust.

A different avenue you can take is keeping *yourself* accountable. You can start by writing down goals you want to accomplish and attainable timelines to reach them. I say attainable timelines because you want to give yourself realistic goals that you can accomplish. If you give yourself unrealistic goals and don't reach them, it can be deflating. The enemy also will tempt your mind to try and give you a million reasons why you should give up.

Reject his lies and keep reminding yourself of the truth that you can do it. Keeping realistic goals and timelines will help eliminate unnecessary distractions.

I will tell you the truth: It's going to take determination and time. If you're expecting a quick fix, you won't get it. Just like someone trying to run a marathon, there are no quick fixes. It takes time, practice, and determination.

WHAT DOES DISCIPLINE HAVE TO DO WITH WORTH?

Perhaps you're wondering why we are talking about discipline. It's not something you hear a lot about, but there's purpose behind it!

Through this book, you've been working through:
- Learning who you are
- Loving who God made you
- Understanding your purpose in His plan
- Discovering your worth and value in Christ

Those are *undoubtedly* the most important, practical things you will ever learn to live out a life of discipleship and freedom. Without that foundation, nothing else you do after that matters. First, you heal the brokenness and the lies you've believed, and then you re-establish your mind in the truth. There are so many things we are called to do as disciples of Christ, like witnessing and loving others. But we cannot love others and do what we are called to do if we aren't first solid in our understanding of our identity because from our identity in Christ flows *everything* else.

Discipline isn't about losing weight, being perfect, or fitting yourself into a mold that the culture tells you you need to fit into. It's about loving who God made you but also taking good care of the temple He gave you. Part of that is disciplining your body and mind to partner with your disciplined and healthy spirit. Remember, we are body, mind, and spirit; they're not separate. Discipline breeds good things in your life in all three areas.

A disciplined mind is a strong mind, and the enemy will do everything he can to convince you that you shouldn't be disciplined, that discipline isn't fun, that it's unnecessary, that it won't produce anything good in your life, or that it's just too hard. He will try everything he can to convince you of this and more. Don't be surprised when you start to discipline yourself if you find yourself questioning if this is really the way to go or if it's really necessary to keep going. That, my friend, is the *most* important time to keep going because it means the enemy is working hard to keep you from something good. He doesn't want good for you; he only wants harm for you. God, on the other hand, only wants good for you. So when the enemy sees you doing something in your life that is going to benefit you, he will try to put thoughts in your mind to keep you from the good. That is *proof* that you're on exactly the right path.

Being disciplined means you also need to allow moments of flexibility. You don't want to become stringent and inflexible. Be spontaneous here and there for things like skipping workouts to be with your kids on a family holiday. Enjoy a slice of cake at a birthday party. Stay up late on New Year's Eve if that's your thing. Be spontaneous because spontaneity is a gift and something to be enjoyed.

Discipline isn't about being strict all the time and never having fun; it's about doing the hard thing now that will produce a harvest later.

We live in a culture that's obsessed with comfort, obsessed with ease, obsessed with rejecting the hard and doing what "feels good." That kind of life is possible, but it won't produce fruit in your life. Producing fruit in your life requires pruning, and pruning is doing the right thing and the hard thing now that will produce the good harvest later.

Anything worth doing takes work—everything from training for a marathon to writing a book. It will take time, energy, determination, and discipline.

Leading a disciplined life means you're preparing now for what you want later. It isn't popular, and it's not always fun, but it *is* worth it. I believe it's part of a balanced life, and it's something that you need to start incorporating into your life. Start small and work your way up, but either way, start. See the areas that need work, and make a goal to put some disciplines in there to help you reach your goals. It can be with food, exercise, sleep, work, family, screen time—you name it!

CHAPTER TEN

In the Middle

I recently had to get braces—as an adult. Ugh. Yup. I'm sure you're all very jealous (insert laughing eye-roll here). Joking aside, although it wasn't something I wanted to do, thankfully, the Invisalign made it more tolerable. It was an almost two-year-long process that I underwent, not for cosmetic reasons, but to help with some spacing issues I was having post-wisdom teeth removal. I'm sure that's a lot more about my teeth than you ever expected (or wanted) to know, but there you have it.

Through the process of moving my teeth around, there were a lot of things I didn't understand; the mechanics of it all were beyond me.

Through the first few months, my teeth began moving in what seemed to me like odd directions. Had you asked me why certain teeth moved in certain directions, I wouldn't have been able to tell you why. Teeth that I thought were going to move didn't, and it created large gaps in-between my bite that made it challenging to chew properly.

I would feel some areas of my teeth moving but not others. The teeth I expected to move first didn't move. Pressure was put on certain teeth that didn't seem to need to move. The entire process was perplexing to me. I expected they were going to do what they were designed to do, but I really didn't understand the process. In the middle of it all, it seemed like nothing was doing what it was supposed to, and I began to feel frustrated.

I was a few months into the process, and I had an appointment coming up. I was going to use it to ask the orthodontist some questions about why things weren't working for me and why things were moving the way they were. I started to wonder if something wasn't right with the aligners and that's why things were feeling weird. In fact, I was almost sure that must be the issue. I felt like I needed understanding to help get me through to the end, because from where I was in the process, it didn't feel right or make sense.

On my way to my appointment, armed with all my questions, I quietly heard the Holy Spirit say to trust the process. I pondered that. It was just a few simple questions I wanted answers to, and although I'm sure my orthodontist would have happily answered my questions, God used a very practical situation to teach me a pivotal lesson about trust. God was trying to teach me something grander than my insignificant problem, something bigger, something deeper, in my walk with Him.

God began revealing to me what it can feel like—being in the middle—and how the middle can be confusing because nothing looks like it's working. In the middle, things don't quite make sense; they're confusing as to the how and why of it all. Yet, if we hold on and trust the process, God can work it all together for our good. He impressed upon my heart how that relates to my walk with Him. When I question God in the middle of the process when He's not quite done yet, and it looks bleak, I'm expecting to see the end results before it's time. But if I can just hold on until the end, I'll see how it all worked out for my good.

I did trust that the orthodontist knew what he was doing, but *I* wanted to understand—to know—for it to make sense to *me*. The outcome wasn't dependent on my understanding of the process, yet, like so many things in life, we *just want to know*—perhaps seeking knowledge as a way to control.

God revealed to me that for the orthodontist to do his job, I didn't need to know how it worked; I just needed to trust the person who knew what to do. My understanding of why my teeth were moving certain ways wouldn't have made the process of moving teeth any better or worse. It wouldn't have changed the outcome. It wouldn't likely even have made sense to me. It just would have given me what I wanted: knowledge. But if I instead trusted the man in charge—the orthodontist—then I didn't need to know the answers. I could trust in *his* skill and ability to make it happen, regardless of my understanding. My understanding wouldn't make one bit of difference in the outcome.

This paralleled so perfectly with what we go through as believers. Oftentimes, when we go through something hard or something we don't understand, we struggle. We don't have the answers. It doesn't make sense. It doesn't happen the way we think it should. It's not in our plan or design. We think it should be another way, yet it isn't. And in the middle of the process is where we can begin to doubt God, doubt His plan, doubt His ways, and doubt the process He's putting us through, but in the middle, we aren't necessarily supposed to have all the answers. In the middle is where it makes the least sense. In the middle is where we are formed and shaped. In the middle is where we can learn to trust God because we don't know the end from the beginning, and we don't know the design plan He has. In the middle is where we grow, both in our trust and faith in God.

Trust the process!

Just like I had to trust the orthodontist that his knowledge would make it all turn out how it was supposed to, we get the chance to trust in God that He's got a good plan for us. We don't need to know how it all works for us to trust Him. We don't need to have the plan all worked out or know the reasons why in order to believe that His plan is good and that He's working it out for *our* good. We can trust that the One who designs our plan and path has it figured out, and we can follow along with Him through the process—because He knows what He's doing even if we don't!

We don't know how it's going to look—only God does. Rather than get frustrated in wanting to understand and wanting God to answer all our questions about *why* He has us in the process or why He designed it that way, we need to stop, pause, and remind ourselves to trust *Him* in the process. Trust Him in the middle. Trust that He knows what He's doing because He does. Trust that He can work it for your good, because He will. That's a promise (Romans 8:28).

Many times in life, we are in the process of learning hard lessons and going through difficult circumstances. You're likely in the middle of a process right now—or perhaps a few. Maybe you're wondering why you're struggling through a health issue, or weight issues, or insecurity, or an accident that left you changed, or any plethora of things. Maybe you've gone through this process, and you feel it's gone on too long. You may feel there's no *way* good can come out of this, or you may even feel it wasn't supposed to be this way. But if you're still here, you are here for a purpose. You're just in the middle right now, but I can promise you that as you continue to give it to Him, He will continue to work on your problem as you work through the process. And maybe, just maybe, the thing that is masquerading as your problem is actually the thing that will lead you to your greatest victory.

THE PROCESS

We know that God is always good and that He can work hard situations out for our good. We don't always see or understand the process (much like the braces), but He is using the circumstances of our lives to build faith, strength, courage, fortitude, and many other things, if we lean into Him, trust Him, ask Him what we should learn from the situation, and allow Him to work it all out for our good. It's so important to remember to also *rest in Him* while going through the process because we need that gentle rest and peace that only He offers, while we are going through the battle. God is always good, and we can have faith in His goodness in our lives while we are in the middle of the process.

When we think of the goodness of God, perhaps when we really get down to it, we think it means that our lives should only be happy and joyful. We shouldn't confuse God's goodness with only positive experiences. Not only do we not see the whole picture the way that God does, but many times, God will use hardship and trials to chip away the fleshly desires and refine us into more holy vessels. Just because something is hard doesn't mean it's from the devil. Just because something is hard doesn't mean God isn't using it for your good. Just because something is hard doesn't mean God's not in it or that we can't trust Him. God uses hard things, too, but He only ever does it to work it out for our good. We see this echoed in Scripture:

> *For the foolishness of God is wiser than men, and the weakness of God is stronger than men. For consider your calling, brothers: not many of you were wise according to worldly standards, not many were powerful, not many were of noble birth. But God chose what is foolish in the world to shame the wise; God chose what is weak in the world to shame the strong. (1 Corinthians 1:25–27)*

> *Can anything ever separate us from Christ's love? Does it mean he no longer loves us if we have trouble or calamity, or are persecuted, or hungry, or destitute, or in danger, or threatened with death? (As the Scriptures say, "For your sake we are killed every day; we are being slaughtered like sheep.") No, despite all these things, overwhelming victory is ours through Christ, who loved us. (Romans 8:35–37)*

As a parent, when your child is misbehaving, do you just let them continue doing the wrong thing, or do you correct their behaviour? Hopefully, you correct their behaviour because you know that they will become unhappy, spoiled children who turn into unhappy adults who can't function with other adults if their behaviour goes left unchecked. Much in the same way, God uses hard circumstances as an opportunity for us to grow in character and grow in learning how to be more like Him—compassionate, trusting, faithful. It may be hard in the middle, but He knows the beginning of the process from the end. He knows what we can handle, and it says in 1 Corinthians 10:13 that He will never allow more to come upon us than what we can bear, but for every temptation (that is common to man), He will provide the way out.

When we trust our circumstances to God, we don't need to be left with the stains of our pain as a residue on our hearts; instead, we are offered an incredible blessing after our trial:

Not only that, but we rejoice in our sufferings, knowing that suffering produces endurance, and endurance produces character, and character produces hope, and hope does not put us to shame, because God's love has been poured into our hearts through the Holy Spirit who has been given to us. (Romans 5:3–5)

And after you have suffered a little while, the God of all grace, who has called you to his eternal glory in Christ, will himself restore, confirm, strengthen, and establish you. (1 Peter 5:10)

Look at just *those* promises alone, and yet, there are many more (Romans 8:28; 2 Corinthians 12:9; Philippians 4:6, 11–13; James 1:3–5, 12)!

We fool ourselves into thinking that walking out the Christian life will not come with hardships along the way or that we are somehow immune. Look at *all* the heroes of faith in the Bible. Shadrach, Meshach, and Abednego faced a fiery furnace and the threat of death. Daniel faced death in a cage with lions. Abraham was tested to see if he would be obedient in sacrificing his son. David faced being chased by a powerful king who wanted to kill him. Moses faced calamity and the threat of death with Pharaoh. In all these stories, we read that God protected and took care of all of His children. Added to that, through those trials, they grew in faith and grew in their ability to trust God. Their faith didn't grow through living a cushy life.

While they were living out those stories—in the middle of the process—they didn't have the luxury of knowing it was all going to work out like we do in reading their stories. There was no foreseeing the future; they only had God's Word to go on and a trust in Him that they held onto. They didn't get to look ahead and see the outcome of their struggles and know it was all going to work out. But

God took care of each of their problems, and He will take care of yours, too. And in exchange, He will give you more faith, more trust in Him, more endurance and fortitude, and more joy, as it says in the Scriptures above. I have seen it not only in Scripture but also in my own life —every time, without fail, that promise is fulfilled. That doesn't mean I always have the answers or know why something is happening, but I always grow when I submit my trial to God.

Because of God's Word, we get to read the stories of our heroes of faith and be encouraged by seeing exactly how God did it—how He used each circumstance and how it all worked together for them. But when they were going through their trials—stuck in the middle of the process— they were holding onto faith that it would be as God said. God's words never return void (Isaiah 55:11), and what He says, He will always do (Ezekiel 24:14) because God cannot lie. When we trust God to work it out and work it out for our good like He says in His Word (Romans 8:28), we can stand in faith and know that if He said it, He *will* do it.

I truly believe that if you asked any one of those heroes of the faith if they would trade what they went through (the trials) for their faith, now, I don't believe a single one of them would. Although hardship is gut-wrenching at times, it also produces growth and faith, and with it, many blessings—as well as a front-row seat to watch the amazing things that God does!

We also have the example of Paul. It says in 2 Corinthians 11:24–28 that Paul faced torture, sickness, jail, and a plethora of other hardships while serving God. Just look at the list:

> *Five times I received from the Jews the forty lashes minus one. Three times I was beaten with rods, once I was pelted with stones, three times I was shipwrecked, I spent a night and a day in the open sea, I have been constantly on the move. I have been in danger from rivers, in danger from bandits, in danger from my fellow Jews, in danger from Gentiles; in danger in the city, in danger in the country, in danger at sea; and in danger from false believers. I have labored and toiled and have often gone without sleep; I have known hunger and thirst and have often gone without food; I have been cold and naked. Besides everything else, I face daily the pressure of my concern for all the churches. (NIV)*

Nowhere in those verses does it say he had it easy—in fact, it says just the opposite—yet we can see how all those trials brought him closer to God, built his faith, and made him strong. In fact, as he points out in 2 Corinthians 12:6–10, he was given a thorn in the flesh, which he believes God allowed in his life to keep him from being proud of all the great works he was doing for the

Kingdom. Paul had *an immense* faith and trust in God, not just because of what he saw God doing, but because of what was being formed inside of him from what he went through: faith, endurance, steadfastness, fortitude. And he went through each trial with the strong faith that he could get through *anything* with God as his strength:

> *But he said to me, "My grace is sufficient for you, for my power is made perfect in weakness." Therefore I will boast all the more gladly about my weaknesses, so that Christ's power may rest on me. That is why, for Christ's sake, I delight in weaknesses, in insults, in hardships, in persecutions, in difficulties. For when I am weak, then I am strong. (2 Corinthians 12:9–10 NIV)*

Throughout his journeys and trials, he learned so much that he was able to put into practice. He says in Philippians 4:11–13:

> *Not that I am speaking of being in need, for I have learned in whatever situation I am to be content. I know how to be brought low, and I know how to abound. In any and every circumstance, I have learned the secret of facing plenty and hunger, abundance and need. I can do all things through him who strengthens me.*

This man was a powerhouse of faith, and he had a strong belief in God to get him through whatever he was facing. He didn't rely on feelings and emotions. He learned what he did by *going through* the hard things and trusting God to deliver him from them. He didn't learn what he learned through cushy, easy circumstances; he learned by being refined in the fire.

REFINEMENT BY FIRE—OUCH!

The process of refinement can be incredibly rewarding at the end, but in the middle, man, it can be messy! God often uses the pain of the process to bring about the beauty of the vessel.

We sing about God being our refiner, we pray and ask Him to refine us, but we say it so haphazardly that perhaps we don't fully understand the meaning behind our request. Do we really know what we are saying when we ask God to refine us?

Metal, before it is melted, can be left the way it is; however, it's not nearly as valuable, beautiful, or precious. It is also not nearly as strong and durable before the refining process. The refining process removes all the impurities and, in turn, creates a metal that is more beautiful, valuable, and durable.

Impurities are removed by exposing the metal to high temperatures. The higher the temperature, the more of the impurities are removed. Each time the heat is turned up, the silversmith skims the impurities off the top and then turns the heat up further to remove more impurities. During each step of the refining process, different kinds of impurities are removed. As the temperature is increased, more types of impurities rise to the top so they can be skimmed off and removed.

The silversmith needs to keep a close eye on the metal as it goes through the process to know when it's finished. He knows that all the impurities are removed when he can see his own reflection in the melted metal. When the impurities are present, they distort the image, but the more they are removed, the more clearly the image becomes of the maker until it's a perfectly clear reflection.

Once the metal has finished its process in the fire, it's pure and complete. It is more durable, has greater value, and is less susceptible to external factors such as corrosion. Without the refining process, the metal would be less stable, weaker, and more susceptible to tarnishing.

Although metal is not alive, nor has any feelings, if we were to imagine what that would feel like, we can imagine it would be painful. Being melted, heated, and then molded would not feel good.

When we look at the refining process that metal goes through, it represents a beautiful analogy of the refining process God does in our life. We see this refining process in Scripture. Psalm 66:10 says, *"For you, God, tested us; you refined us like silver"* (NIV). (See also Proverbs 17:3; 1 Peter 1:6–7.)

We start off like the metal: fit for use but imperfect. The imperfections of sin and fleshly desires make us weak and more susceptible to tarnishing (hardships). God knows it's important to remove the impurities (sin, fleshly desires, wrong thinking) in our lives because afterward, it allows us to be more complete, more holy, and more like Him. But the only way to experience those things is on the other side of the process—the refining process. We cannot experience those things without going through the fire. He lovingly turns the heat up in order to remove the impurities in our lives. And as He slowly skims off the impurities, we begin to reflect His image. Over time, more impurities are removed, and we begin to act more like Him, talk more like Him, think more like Him, and reflect His character.

We go through more than just one refining process through our journey of life. We are in a continual process of renewal and refinement, but God only brings us through what He knows we can handle and when we are ready. Through the process, He doesn't take His eye (or His hand) off of us. He takes us through the journey each time, never leaving or forsaking us. Yes, it's hard and messy, but after it's all said and done, we are more pure, more durable to face life's challenges, and we reflect more of our Saviour's image.

I've referred to this verse before, but I want to point us back to Romans 8:28. Most of us know what Romans 8:28 promises, and we often hear it quoted when someone is going through something hard: *"And we know that in all things God works for the good of those who love him, who have been called according to his purpose"* (NIV). You may know it and be able to quote it, but *do you believe it?* Do you believe that it's true no matter what comes your way? Do you believe that God will bring you through it? It's easy to confidently stand and believe in that truth while life is smooth sailing, but when we're stuck in the middle of it all, do we waver in faith and let doubt begin to creep in?

When confronted with hardship, I have had many times when I've held strong to my faith despite my circumstances, but I'll be honest in saying I've also had moments when I've doubted, wondered, and worried. Thankfully, by God's grace, He is steady in helping remind me, comfort me, and give me faith to pick myself back up and try again.

AN UNUSUAL SIDE-EFFECT

Imagine for a moment if what you're facing could be part of the plan God is using in your life to propel you forward. What if God allowed you to go through this hardship because He knew it would bring something good in your life, some kind of spiritual growth or victory? What if this journey is exactly what you needed so you could be set free from something that's been holding you back for a long time? Does that change how you see your journey?

When I first began this journey of understanding my identity almost five years ago, I vividly remember looking back at old photos of myself and envying what I had when I was younger. I pined after the plump skin that so softly picked up the sunset as it danced across my cheek, the smaller-sized jeans that didn't pinch and pucker at the waistband, and the freshness in my smile that wasn't dragged down with life's worries. I remember how I felt when I would look back at old photos of myself, and I would feel gutted, angry, and sad after seeing them. I longed for what I no longer had because my worth was still defined by external things, and those external things had changed.

I questioned why on earth I was so hard on myself back then when I was younger, thinner, "prettier" by the world's standards. What on earth did I have to complain about? But I did complain. All the time. Not to anyone else but to myself. The dialogue I had with myself wasn't kind in the least. I had not felt the least bit good about myself back then, despite having then what I would have dreamed to have when I was going through my weight gain. I had wasted that time back then, thinking I needed to be something more, something better, something else.

Even back then, when I looked thinner than I do now, younger than I do now, I was still unhappy with myself. When I was struggling through my journey, before God helped set me free and taught me who I am, I would have done anything to go back in time and reclaim what once was. All those years ago, I hadn't really yet understood where my worth came from; I was still muddling through it all.

My twenty-five-year-old, thin self still thought she needed to lose ten more pounds, lose the puckers in her skin, and have thighs that didn't rub together or jiggle when she walked in a swimsuit on the beach—all the things that she thought mattered so much were but only a breath (Psalm 144:4; Ecclesiastes 1:2). Twenty-five-year-old me missed out on enjoying certain activities or seasons in life because she longed for a better version of her body that didn't exist, a better version that alluded her, a better version that was always *just* out of reach.

Even then, she wasn't happy and wanted better. If my twenty-five-year-old self knew what she'd look like as her thirty-nine-year-old self, what would she have thought of her future self? Would she have torn her apart, wrinkle by wrinkle, sag by sag, pant size by pant size, and hoped for something different?

But what my twenty-five-year-old self doesn't know is my thirty-nine-year-old self loves who she is now, and no amount of exterior renovation will make her any *more*, or any *less*, happy. What that younger, thinner, more toned, and perkier self didn't know was that the older version of herself wouldn't let her body define her worth anymore. She would learn through trials, hardship, fire, and drought, that her worth wasn't tied up in all the things she thought it was. It was tied up in the One who never changes, the One who defined her from the moment she was a twinkle in her mother's eye. What she didn't know then, she knows now, and she's been set free in that knowledge.

When thirty-nine-year-old me looks back at old photos now, do you know what she sees? She sees joy in that moment in time. She recognizes the smiles on her kid's faces from splashing around in the water with their mama. She sees her family growing from little babies to young women, and she feels incredibly blessed. She is reminded of that funny comment caught on camera that made them laugh, or that exciting experience they had, or that moment of impact that plays like an old-fashioned movie reel in her mind. She doesn't wish for any of her old body back because it made her who she is today. She doesn't pine for the smaller self, the thinner self, the younger self —she instead sees all the moments of joy captured by the quick click of a button.

Thirty-nine-year-old me doesn't even look back at twenty-five-year-old me and wish she could teach her then what she knows now because it's through the hard times that she actually grew, not through the easy ones. But thirty-nine-year-old me does desire to give all the wisdom from her journey to the other twenty-five, nineteen, thirty-nine, fifty-three, and ninety-nine-year-olds and everyone in-between—the truth and knowledge about who they are, who God made them to be, and where exactly their worth and value are found.

Don't waste a single day more pining for what once was, or what you used to look like, or want to look like. Don't let that be a reason not to love who you are and the season you're in—don't let it define you.

Rarely, if ever, are we fully satisfied with where we are at because human nature is constantly looking for the next best thing, but we don't have to give in. Don't believe the lie that you'll be happy *when*. You'll be happy *when* your promotion comes through. You'll be happy *when* you get that proposal and can be his wife. You'll be happy *when* you lose twenty pounds. You'll be happy *when* you get rid of those wrinkles. *Embrace who you are right now.* Look for what God has for you, here and now. Take stock of your life and all the joy and beauty that's around you, and embrace it. Work on yourself inside, asking the Holy Spirit to help direct and guide you, and thank God for His goodness to help you get through all the things ahead. There is so much goodness that God has given you in your life right now—pay attention to it! And before long, you'll find that you don't have to look so hard anymore.

As we close our journey together, I want to leave you with these thoughts.

Look back on the journey God's taken you through. The old is gone, and the new has come. That person is a girl you used to know, someone you remember but someone you no longer know.

You now know your true identity and who you are. It's no longer what you used to think it was: your job, your wealth, your looks—whatever you wore as a robe. God showed you your old identity so He could robe you in your new identity—your true identity in Him. This process has unearthed the things that needed to be released, brought into the light the things that needed to be healed, and allowed you to let them go. Like a bird being set free, you can let go of the old self, because you know that you can now walk in the true identity of who God made you: a vessel for honourable use.

You can take with you the lessons that you've learned; after all, you wouldn't be where you are without them, so honour what the past has taught you, and thank God for the process that brought you to where you are now. Embrace the next season with arms wide open, ready to receive whatever else God has in store for you.

With that, I encourage you, dear friend, to continue on, fighting the good fight of faith and resting in the truth that your pant size doesn't define you, God does.

Notes

1. James Gant, "She had a lovely sense of humor," *Dailymail.com*, September 9, 2022, https://www.dailymail.co.uk/news/article-11193985/Her-Majestys-humor-Queen-PRANKED-two-American-tourists.html.

2. Andy Cook, "Sermon: Called to be a Super-Champion," *Lifeway.com*, January 1, 2014, https://www.lifeway.com/en/articles/sermon-champions-conuqerors-romans-8.

3. Bill Johnson, *Dreaming With God* (Destiny Image Publishers, 2006), 56.

4. Johnson, *The Supernatural Power of a Transformed Mind* (Destiny Image Publishers, 2014), 105.

5. Brandon Wall, Oasis City.

6. Attributed to Alexander Hamilton, *Forbes.com*, accessed October 23, 2024, https://www.forbes.com/quotes/254/.

7. Joyce Meyer, *Battlefield of the Mind: Winning the Battle in Your Mind* (Warner Books, 1995).

8. Attributed to Hillary Morgan Ferrer, *Mama Bear Apologetics* (Harvest House Publishers, 2019).

9. Craig Groeshel, *Winning the War in Your Mind: Change Your Thinking, Change Your Life* (Zondervan, 2021), 1.

10. "The Ass in the Lion's Skin," *Fables of Aesop*, July 4, 2016, https://fablesofaesop.com/the-ass-in-the-lions-skin.html.

11. Fabiola R., "Discipline Pays Off: The Pain of Discipline Versus the Pain of Regret," April 18, 2023, https://www.linkedin.com/pulse/discipline-pays-off-pain-versus-regret-fabiola-riobe/.